Oleg Pomoshnikov

The Soviet Skoryi Class Destroyer

KAGERO

Starboard side view.

Introduction

The „Smelyi" type destroyer, Project 30 bis (Skoryi class, according to NATO classification), was the first destroyer designed and built after World War Two with new shipbuilding technologies available in the USSR.

World War Two demonstrated that all early-built Soviet destroyers had serious flaws. Poor seaworthiness, hull fragility, lack of displacement reserves for modernization. The technical design and working drawings of the new EM were developed under the leadership of the main designer A.L. Fisher. On 28 January 1947, by order of the Council of Ministers of the USSR N3 149-75 „On the construction of destroyers of the 30K and 30 bis Projects", the technical design developed in TsKB-53 was approved.

The construction of ships of this series was to take place at four shipyards: No. 190 in Leningrad (now St. Petersburg), No. 200 in Mikolayov, No. 199 in Komsomolsk-on-Amur and No. 402 in Molotov (now the town of Severodvinsk).

In addition, it was agreed that each of the four shipyards will provide vessels to „its" own fleet, i.e

Plant No. 402 was to build destroyers for the Northern Fleet, the Leningrad No. 190 plant for the Baltic Fleet. The ships from Mikoyov's plant were assigned to the Black Sea Fleet. And plant No. 199 in Komsomolsk-on-Amur provided vessels to the Pacific Fleet.

In total, seventy ships were built in 1949–1953. It was the largest series of Soviet vessels ever built and in such a short time. The whole series was completed in less than five years.

Construction

The Poject 30bis destroyers were a direct development of the Project 30 and 30 K project. But the 30bis, compared to them, had larger dimensions, which improved the ship's stability and managed to get more space for radio-electronics and other equipment.

When commencing creation of the main design of the 30 bis, at that time, the Soviet navy specialists had experience in construction and combat use of the 7, 7U, 30 and 30K destroyers.

In the hull part of the project, the designers of TsKB-53 bureau took into account the experience of the German shipbuilding industry, with which they got acquainted by both captured technical documentation and research of German destroyers inherited from the USSR for repairs.

The shape of the stern, also borrowed from the German destroyers of the 1936-A project, while maintaining a spacious stern, enabled contouring in the area of the constructive line above and below the waterline and underwater to get speed improvement and ease of reverse control.

The design of the fore part changed and got a first-level platform for an additional 37 mm cannon, and the closed navigation bridge, which was considered during the war to be very uncomfortable in controlling the ship in repelling enemy aircraft attacks, gave way to an open one. Protection against wind was to be carried out in a way noticed on German ships - with a special windscreen that directed the air flow upwards, shielding those on the bridge from the oncoming air stream.

For the first time in the USSR, the ship's hull was completely welded.

The process of creating welding technology for the shipbuilding industry had used experience of automated welding in the production of tanks.

So, when developing technology maps for welding hull sections of the ship, the relevant Uralmashzavod documentation served as the pattern.

The total length of welding lines on each ship was about 16 km, and energy consumption was over 150 kWh.

But the achievements did not come immediately. The lack of development of new steel welding technology was one of the reasons for the appearance of cracks in the tensioned structures of ships' hulls. After the first months of operations of the destroyers delivered to the fleet, cracks were found in the aft area. The second reason for their appearance was the lack of rigidity of the frame structures, which had to be strengthened. The correction of this structural defect cost 700,000 roubles per ship. The cost of building a series production ship at that time was about 100 million roubles.

The 30 bis returned to the use of propeller shaft fairings, used for the first time in the domestic shipbuilding industry, to achieve the maximum speed of the project leader. According to the plan, the use of this shape of the drive shaft fairing in the Project 30bis was to ensure a favourable influence of the fairings on the stern flow and their stabilizing effect during turning and tilting. This explains the lack of side keels in both projects that appeared on the overloaded ships of the previous constructions.

The 30bis had typical semi-armoured architecture typical for destroyers. The hull had 17 watertight bulkheads.

According to the technical design, the 30 bis destroyers had a standard displacement of 2,351 tons, a normal displacement of 2,726 tons and a full of 3,101 tons; main dimensions (overall/waterline): length 120.5/116 m, beam 12/11 m, average draft 3.86 m (at normal displacement) and 4.25 m the largest. The speed: maximum - 36.6 knots, technical and economic - 15.7 knots, and operational and economic - 19 knots. The cruising range was 1,000, 3,660 and 3,600 nautical miles, respectively.

Studying the 30bis destroyers, you can see many obvious influences of the German shipbuilding industry.

The keel of the 30bis leading ship was laid on the slipway of the Leningrad shipyard named after A.A. Zhdanov on 16 May 1948, and was given the name „Smelyi".

Launched four and a half months later, she was commissioned after state tests on 21 December 1949. The date coincided with the I.V. Stalin's birthday. Although the Far Eastern "Vstrechnyi's" approval certificate was signed for two weeks only, and the Black Sea ‚Vdelitelnyi", almost two months earlier than the birthday of the party leader, a relatively short construction period was achieved by cross-sectional assembly of the ship's hull, which was built at the construction site with 101 sections. The sections were pre-welded in the assembly hall in special guides - „beds" - and were transported to the slipway and assembled together, quickly forming the ship's hull.

Factory sea trials took place in the Gulf of Finland, and for state tests the destroyer under the command of the Captain 3rd rank I.S. Startsev moved to the Baltic Sea Base. On the morning of 3 November, having aboard the National Acceptance Commission chaired by Rear Admiral N.O. Abramov, the "Smelyi" entered the Gulf of Gdańsk. On the first of December, having spent a total of 145 hours in motion, 10 of them carried out at the maximum speed, after covering 5,250 nautical miles and consumed 3,960 tons of fuel, as well as firing tests, the destroyer entered the stage of a complete check of technical condition by the twentieth day of testing.

The next day, the ship was officially commissioned.

In the approval act, the state commission noted that the ship had developed a full speed of 36.6 knots, i.e. one knot more than specified. The speed was achieved thanks to the strength of the main mechanisms with the output of 60,700 HP and 445 revolutions of propeller shafts per minute, the actual displacement in this case corresponded to normal – 2,691 tons. The cruising range (with a full fuel reserve of 744 tons) was: operational - economical at 19 knots – 3,660 miles, at full speed – 1,000 miles, which also exceeded the expectations. During testing at full speed, the destruction of the hearth of the main KV-30 boilers was noticed. Damages were removed on the spot in accordance with the recommendations of the boiler makers the Plant No. 189. The State Commission drew attention to the noise of the TVK-U turbofans and flooding them by waves, which did not allow the development of speed by more than 28 knots.

When the displacement was less than normal, the ship began to roll, and on the passing wave it strongly „cleared" - deviated from the course by 5-8 degrees. The diameter of the steady-state circulation at full speed - more than eight body lengths - exceeded the required handling characteristics. In the final report, the Commission noted the main disadvantage of the main guns – lack of versatility. The „aggravating circumstance" was the lack of the Mina-30bis system, which did not generate data for anti-aircraft fire, even within the existing elevation, i.e. up to 45 degrees.

The Soyuz-30bis 85mm anti-aircraft fire control system was unable to provide data for firing at diving aircraft. All this, according to the commission, determined „the low efficiency of fulfilling air defense tasks "Smelyi" during the fight against the modern air enemy means".

The final test report on the "Smelyi" noted that at a wave exceeding 18 knots, firing became impossible due to water getting into the trunks of the main calibre bow turret and some AA gun posts were washed over. In April 1951, systematic trials of the 30 bis began in the Black Sea. On „Bystryi" during the next docking, the broadside keels were installed, and on „Bezupretchnnyi" – some fittings on the bridge were added. The seaworthiness of both ships was evaluated and compared. In the autumn of the same year, the destroyer „Otchotlivyi" was tested in the Barents Sea, and the lessons learnt made it possible to draw an exhaustive conclusion about the navigability of the Project 30bis vessels, thus confirming the effectiveness of the actions taken.

A ship is made for battle. Therefore, to eliminate the main disadvantage of the „thirty bis" - the inability of anti-aircraft weapons to cope with a modern air enemy - it was necessary to concentrate all efforts on this flaw.

In effect, the ships were aditionally equipped with twin 37mm V-11 anti-aircraft guns, which were developed before the war and no longer corresponded to the significantly increased level of the air threat, but nevertheless somehow improved firepower.

Port side view.

Power unit

The composition and layout and arrangement of power units as well as auxiliary mechanisms were approximately the same as in the 30K and 30 projects. The location of the boiler room and engine compartment is also similar: two fore boiler rooms - one engine compartment, two feeding boiler rooms, one engine room (feeding).

The main KV-30 steam boilers installed on these EMs belonged to the type of four-manifold water boilers. In the boiler room they had a convection heating surface and air heaters with a fan. Steam parametres behind the superheaters of KV-30 boilers were as follows: 2.8 MPa pressure and 325° C respectively at economic speed.

The TV-6 type were used as the main turbo gears on the 30 bis project destroyers, as well as on the 30K. They developed the output of up to 60,000 litres (full-ahead engine power was 30,000 litres for each such unit), and reverse - 15,000 litres. To transfer torque to the propellers was provided by two drive shafts. Its high reliability besides, the power unit was basically an outdated pre-war development.

Table of main features

Dimensions (m):	
overall	120.5
max. beam	12.0
draft	4.26
Displacement (t):	
standard	2,290
normal	2,665
full	3,040
Engine	4 KV-30 boilers, two TV-6 steam turbines, 60,000 HP, two three-blade propellers.
Speed (knots):	
max.	36.5
economic	16.0
Range (nautical miles)	
full speed	980
economic	3,660
Armament:	two B-2LM turrets, 4-130 mm/50; one universal 92-K mount, 2-85 mm/52; seven 37 mm anti-aircraft guns 70-K or 4x2 37 mm AU V-11.
Machine guns (on early ships):	two 12.7 mm 2M-1 machine guns or four 12.7 mm DShKM
Torpedoes:	two five-tube launchers PTA 53-30bis; 533 mm calibre.
Anti-sumbarine:	2 BMB-1, then 2 BMB-2; 2 bomb throwers (51 depth charges); 52 KB mines or 60 M-26
Electronics:	„Redan - 2"-1; „Wympel"-2 -1; „Fakel-M"-2
Crew:	286 including 19 officers

Armament

The composition of the anti-aircraft systems was made of 2x2-130/50 mm - on-board gun systems B-2-LM (with ammunition supply of 150 shells per barrel); universal mounts for revolver guns 2-85/52 mm 92-K (ammunition - 300 rounds per barrel), as well as 7 automatic anti-aircraft guns 7 37/63 mm 70-K. From 1951, destroyers of the Project 30 bis were given new anti-aircraft guns of the same calibre - B-11. The ammunition supply – 1,200 rounds per barrel. Torpedo armament consisted of two five-tube 53 cm torpedo launchers of the PTA-53-Z0-bis type (supply

- 10 torpedoes) and the Mina-30-bis system. Anti-submarine weapons were provided by two BMB-1 or BMB-2 depth charge launchers, as well as two stern launchers. The destroyers also could lay mines: 52 of the KB type or 60 M-26. Similar to the Project 30K, a radio-technical weapon was mounted – a radar.

There were the Rif-1 surface radars, Redan main gun radar and Vympel-2 anti-aircraft radar. The Rym-1 system was used as the navigational radar station. It should be noted that, in general, both guns and anti-submarine weapons of the Project 30 bis were morally and technically obsolete by the time these ships entered service and did not quite meet the requirements. But due to the installation of new radar detection means and fire control systems, the combat capabilities of these ships were increased.

ORP GROM
1957 -... Commander Second Lieutenant Witold Gliński.
ORP WICHER Commanders
1958–1961: Capt. Henryk Koryciński
• 1961–1965: Cmdr. Andrzej Ujazdowski
• 1965–1969: Cmdr. Tadeusz Moskwa
• 1969–1970: Second Lieutenant Cmdr. Józef Wołczyński
• 1970–1974: Cmdr. Tadeusz Pabiś

Bibliography

V.I. Nikolsky, D. Yu. Litinsky, Yu. V. Apalkov. Torpedo destroyers. 30bis project. „Warships of Russia" series. Historical Maritime Society, 1994

V.P. Zablotsky. Squadrons of destroyers of the Project 30 bis (Part 1), (Maritime collection 2014-06) Modelist. Moscow 2014

V. P. Zablotsky, squadrons of destroyers of the Project 30 bis (Part 2), (Maritime collection 2014-07) Model Designer. Moscow 2014

Mariusz Motyka, Robert Andrzej Jamka. ORP „Wicher II" in "Okręty" Issue No. 8 (9) November 2011, Kagero Publishing

forums.airbase.ru/2008/10/t63959--esminets-pr-30-bis-30-k-tipa-smelyj.html

forums.airbase.ru/2011/08/t87107--eskadrennye-minonostsy-proektov-30k-30-bis-31-i-modifikatsii.html

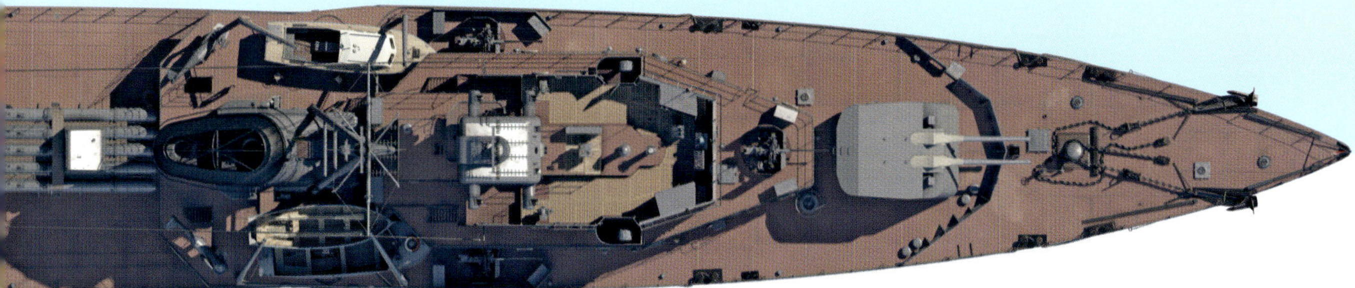

Top view.

Bow view.

Stern view.

Bow port side of the ship with B-2LM turret.

Port side of bow superstructure.

Port side view of the upper part of the bow superstructure and the foremast.

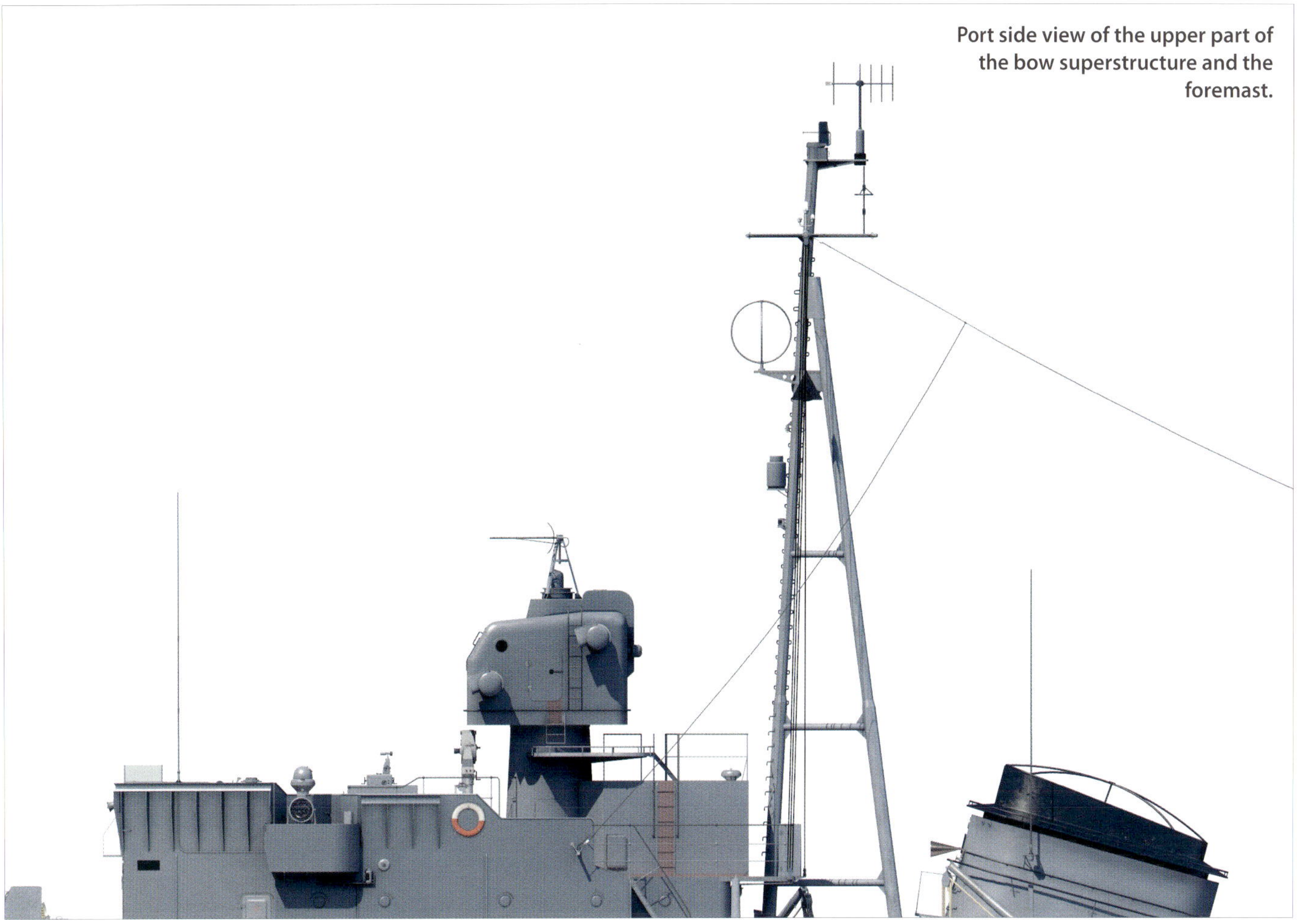

Port side of the midship with the bow PTA-53-30bis 533 mm torpedo launcher and with the mid superstructure.

Port side of the mid superstructure with the aft mast and a stern funnel.

Port side of the stern superstructure.

Stern port side of the ship.

Starboard side view of the bow.

Starboard side of the bow superstructure.

Starboard side of the upper part of the bow superstructure and the foremast.

Starboard side view of the midship.

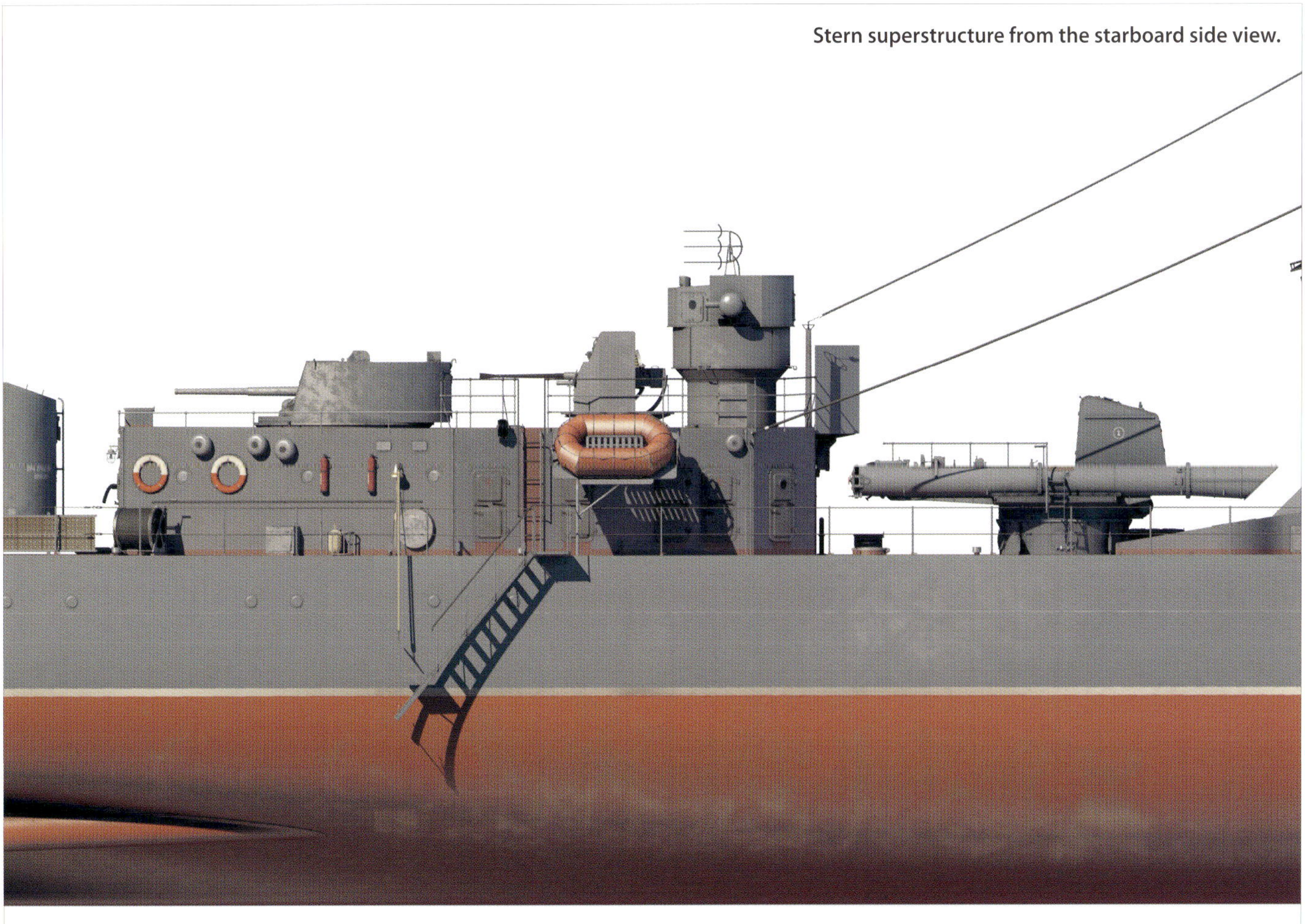

Stern superstructure from the starboard side view.

Starboard stern view, right propeller.

Top view of the bow, breakwater, anchor chains and capstans visible.

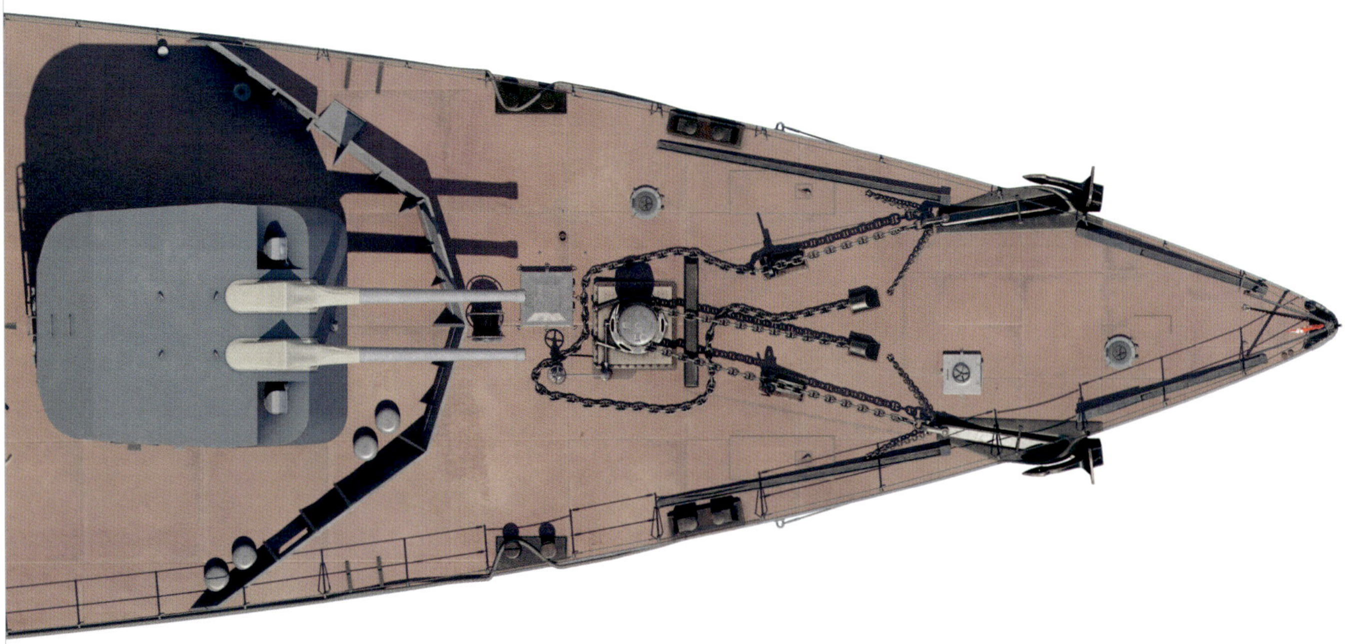

Top view on the captain's bridge.

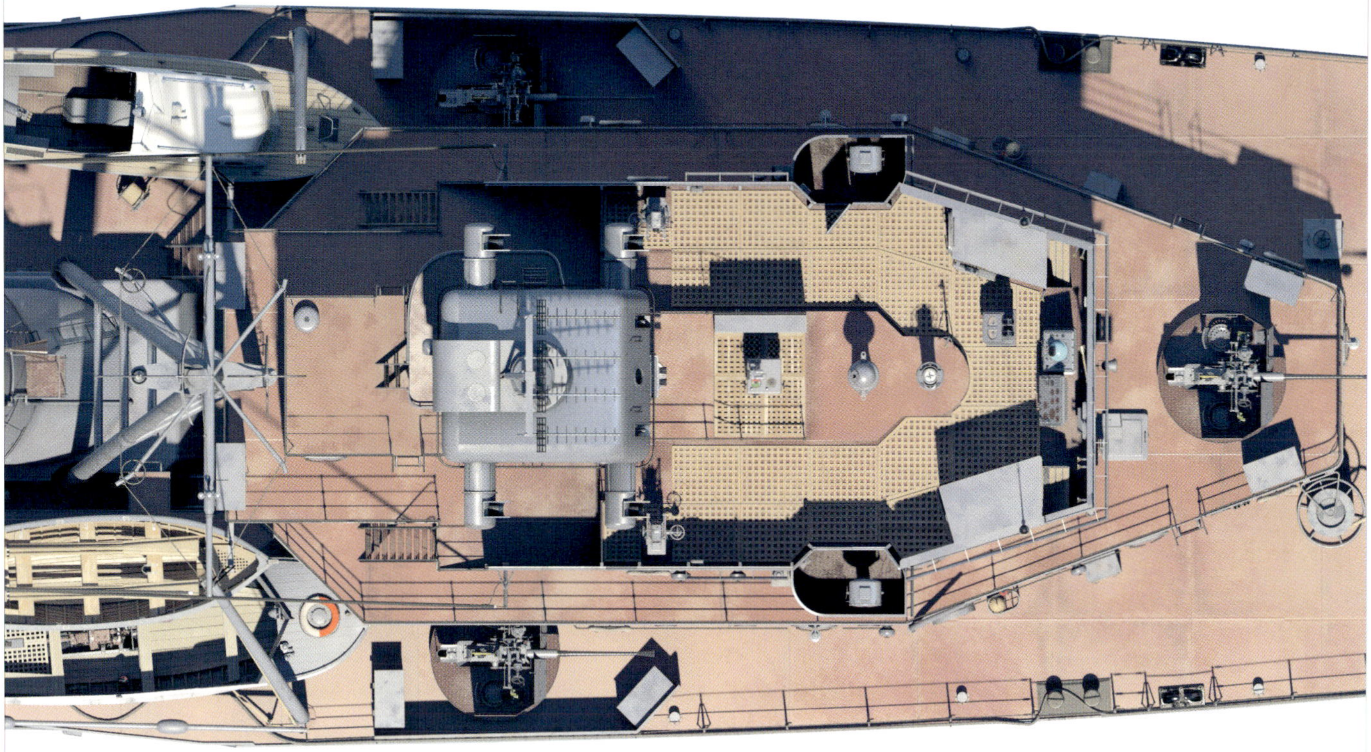

Top view on the bow, funnel and PTA-53-30bis 533 mm torpedo launcher battery.

Top view on the mid superstructure, stern funnel and the second PTA-53-30bis 533 mm torpedo launcher battery.

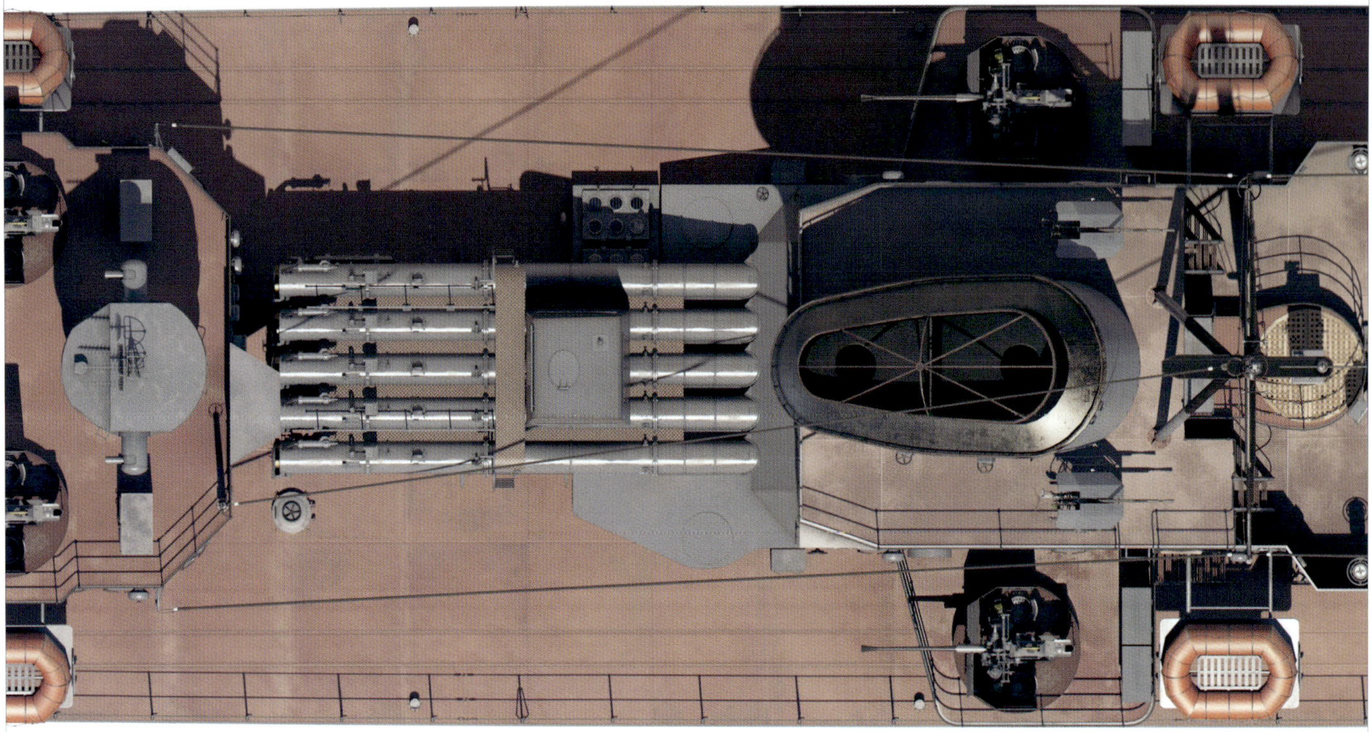

Top view on the stern, superstructure, universal gun mount 92K 2x85mm and two AA gun 70K 37mm.

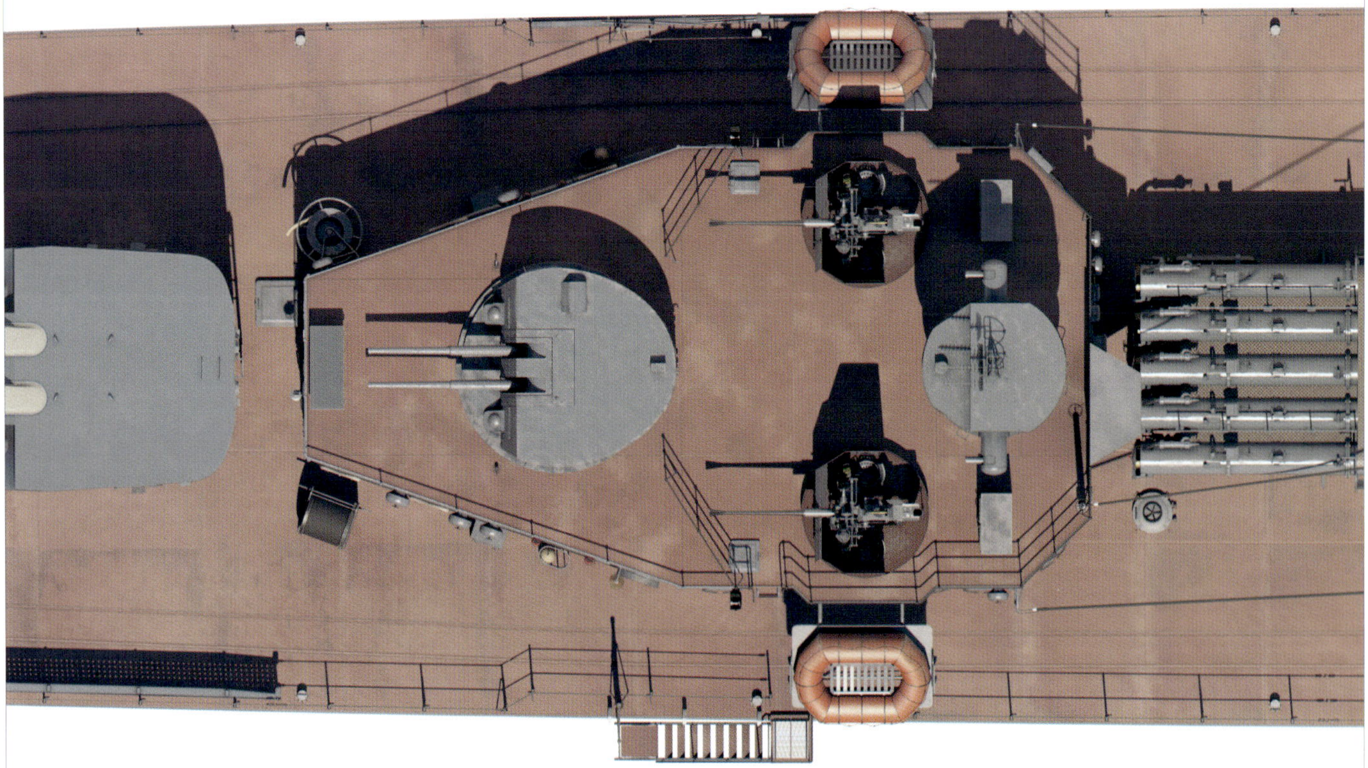

Top view on the stern B-2LM 130mm gun turret and depth charge devices.

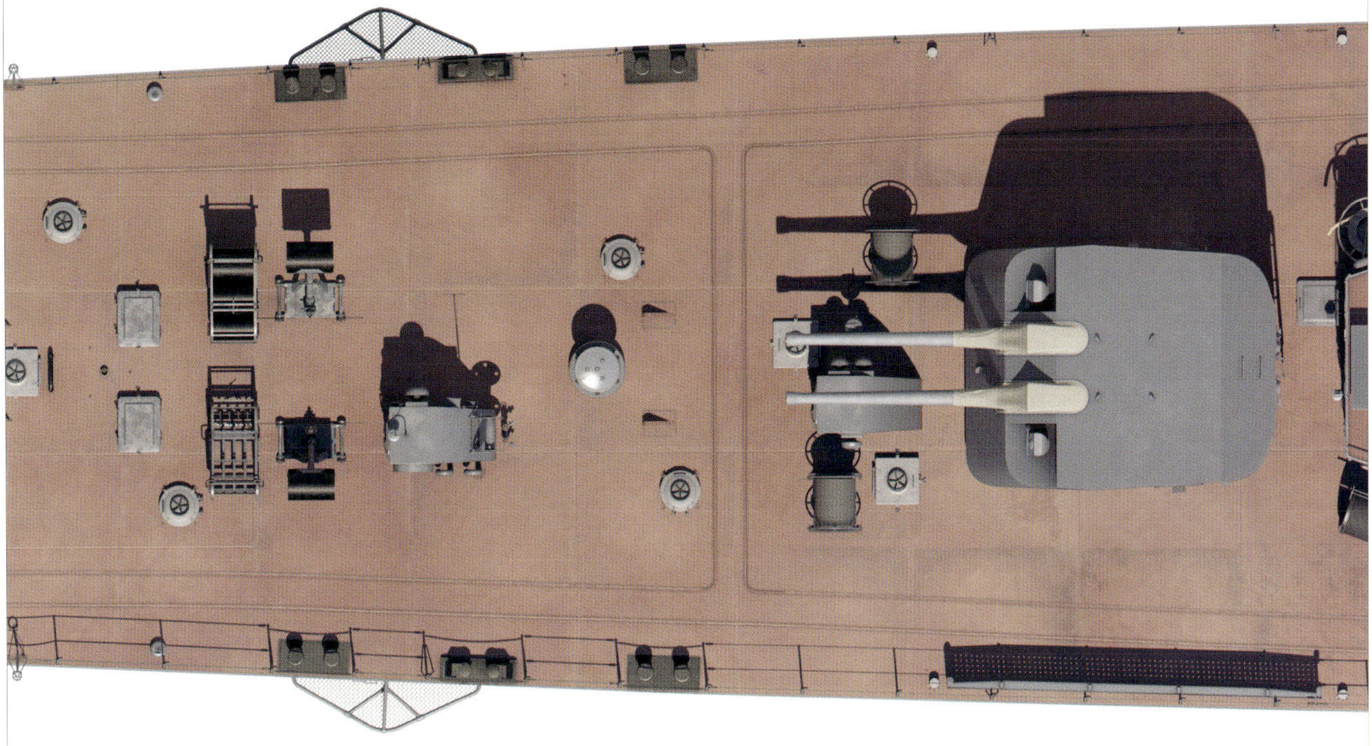

Top view on the stern; BMB-1 depth charge throwers and depth charge racks.

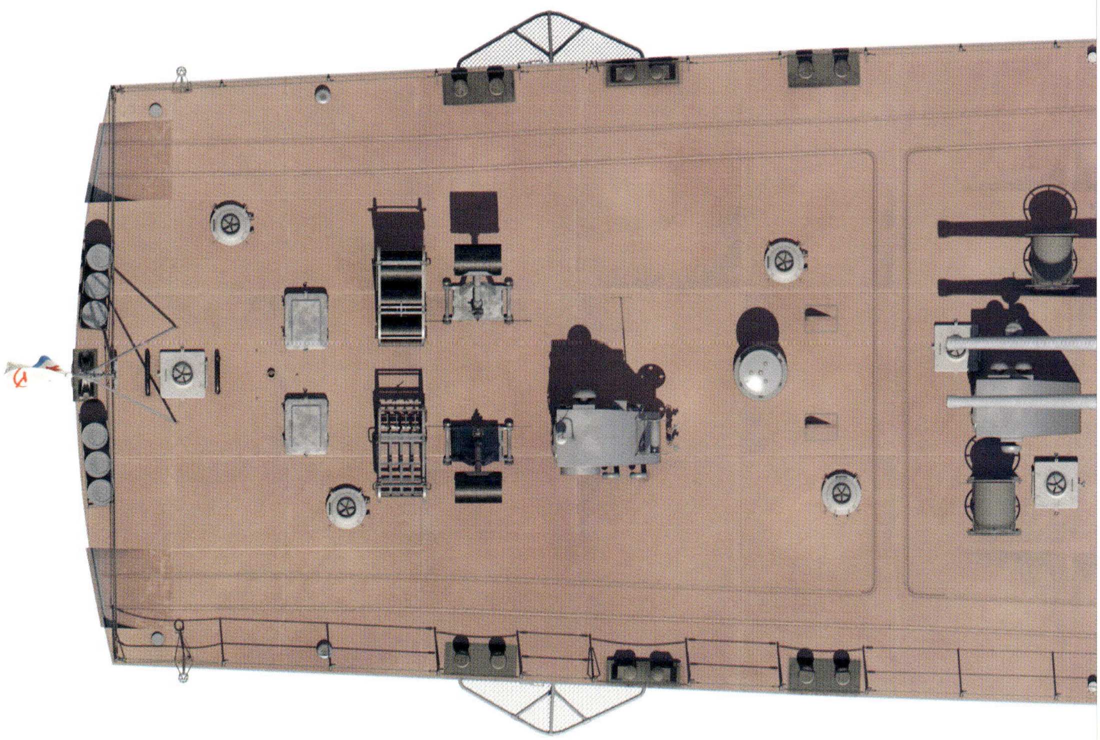

Foredeck.

Anchor chains and the capstans.

Details of the bow part.

The bow main artillery turret.

Port side view of the bow B-2 LM main artillery turret, breakwater and bow AA gun 70K 37mm.

Port side view of the bow AA gun 70K 37mm.

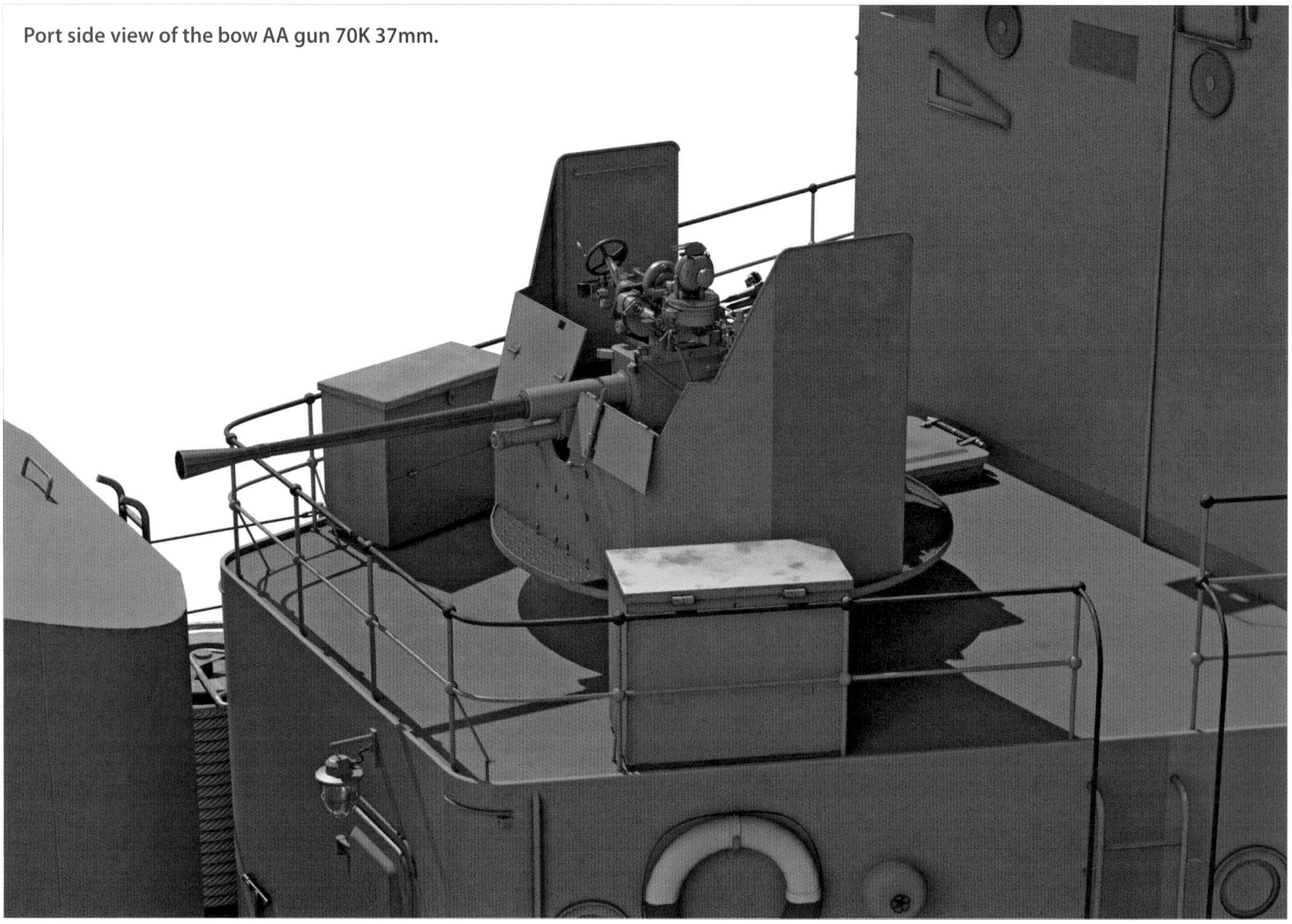

Starboard view of the bow AA gun 70K and back side of the bow main artillery turret.

The right side of the base of the bow superstructure.

The left side of the base of the bow superstructure.

Port side view of the commander bridge.

Starboard side view of the commander bridge.

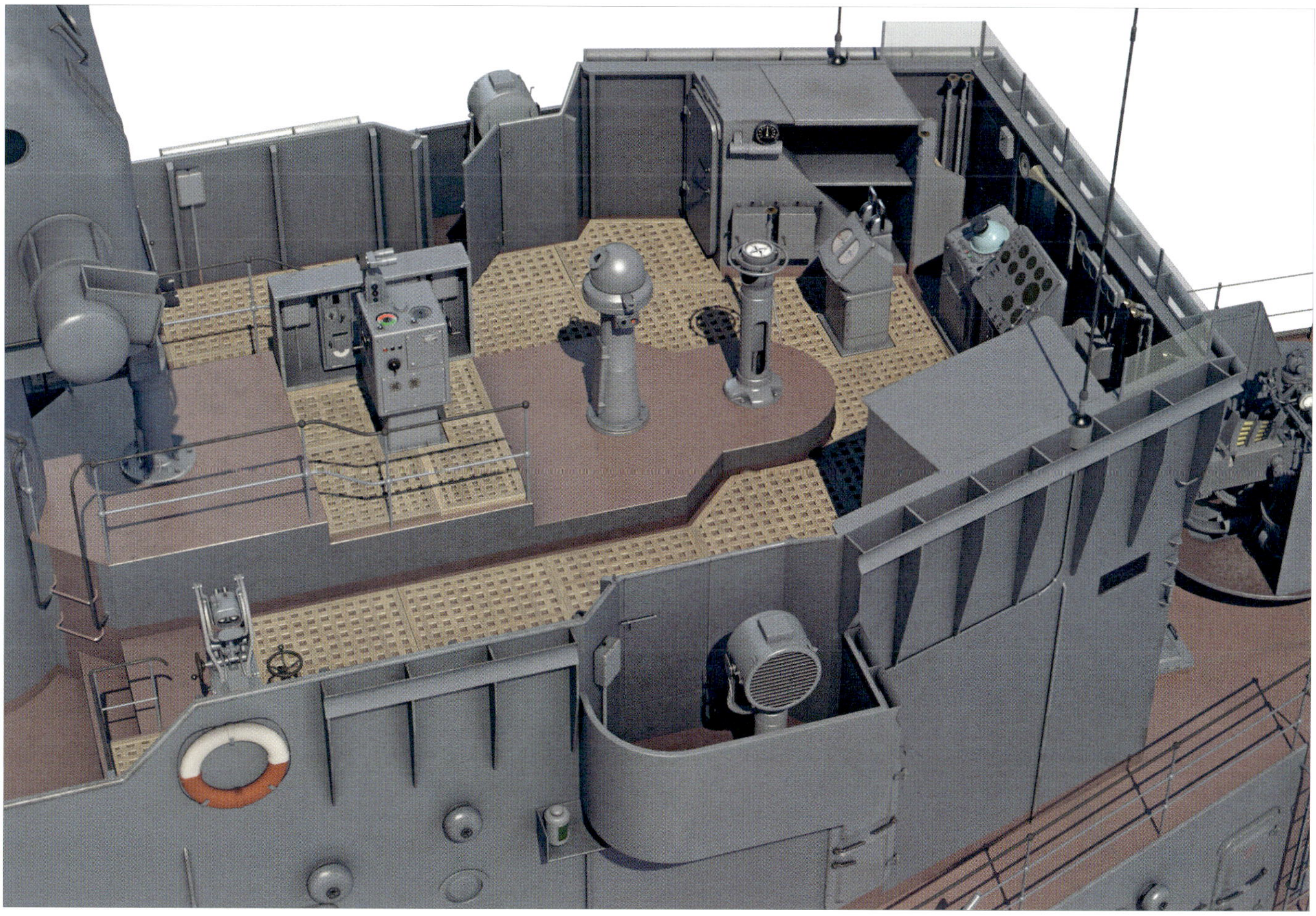

Starboard side, view from top on the commander bridge.

Right side of the commander bridge with WCUZ-1 anti-aircraft target sight.

Interior of the bridge;from the right: torpedo fire control device "Mina-30bis",VIKO- circular view station, machine telegraph, pelorus,gyro repeater.

The bridge details in front part.

Details of the central part of the bridge: gyro repeater, NM-1 night artillery sight, PMR-21 Inclinometer.

Port bridge view; from the left: NM-1 night artillery sight, PMR-21Inclinometer.

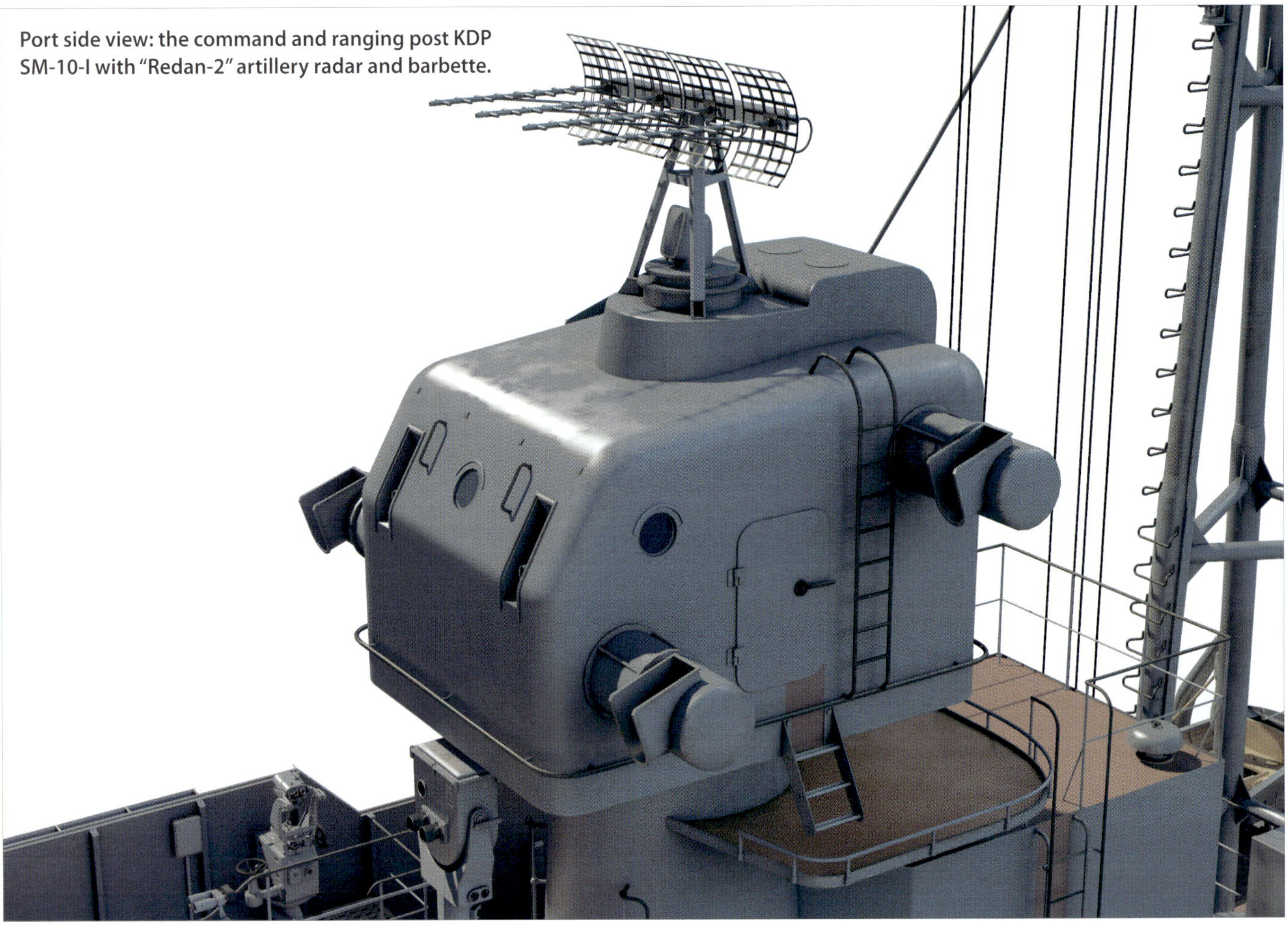

Port side view: the command and ranging post KDP SM-10-I with "Redan-2" artillery radar and barbette.

Starboard side view of the command and ranging post KDP SM-10-I with "Redan-2" artillery radar on the roof of KDP.

Rear view of the KDP SM-10-I with "Redan-2" artillery radar.

Stern view on the bow superstructure and KDP SM-10-I.

Stern left view of the superstructure base and commander boat.

Back view of the superstructure base. Starboard side.

Starboard side view: the bottom of tripod foremast, cover of the bow funnel, six oared yal, work cutter and paravans.

Port side: commander boat, tripod foremast, cowling of the bow funnel and paravans.

Port side view of the bow funnel.

Port side view of the boom to operate the paravane and commander boat and davits.

Stern view of the starboard boom.

Starboard view of the bow funnel.

Starboard side view of the foremast upper part with radio-electronic devices: at the bottom a direction –finder, above on a platform "Ryf-1" radar, behind it "Fakel" Friend or Foe System (IFF) antennas.

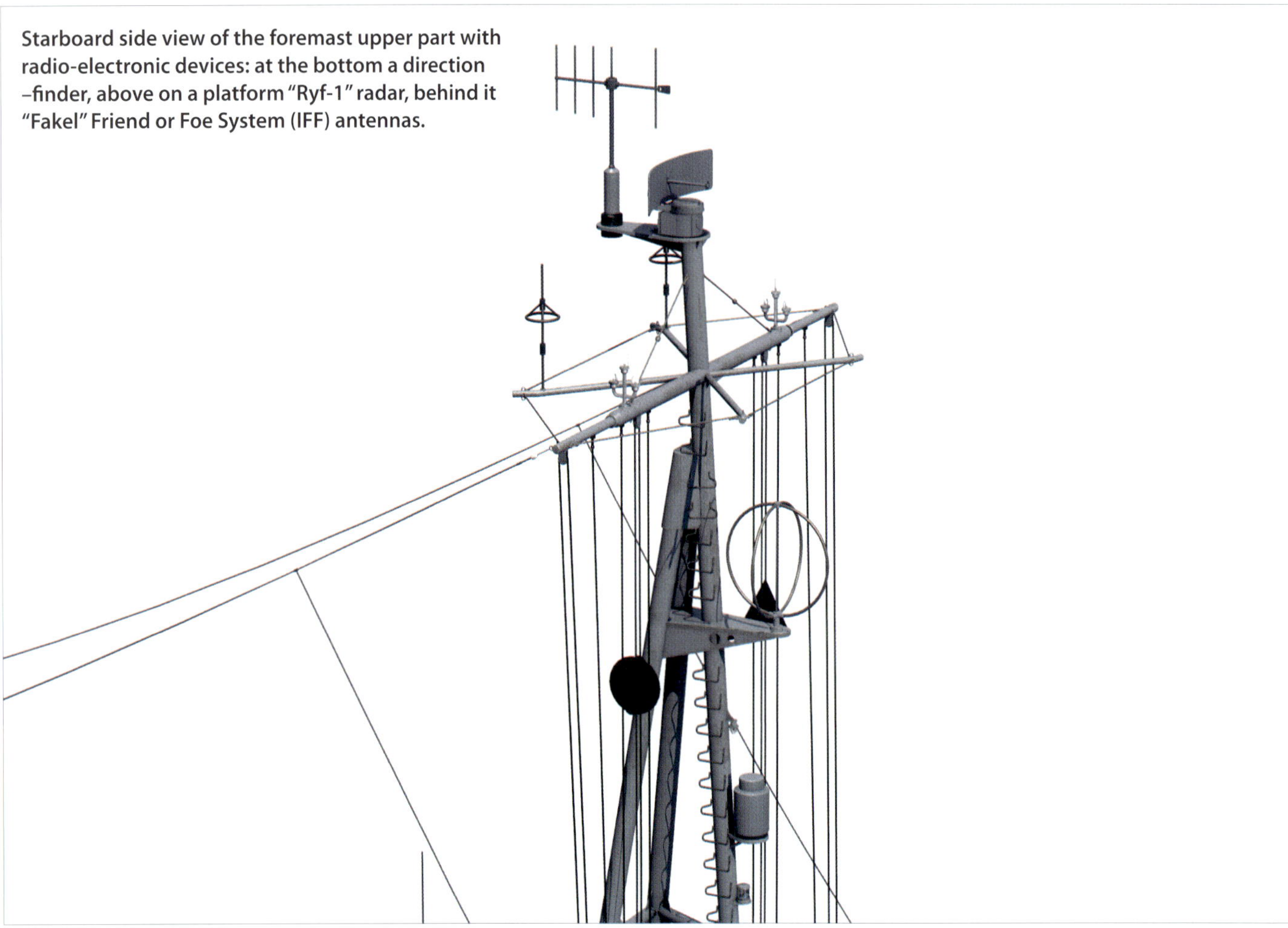

Ryf-1 radar close up view.

Ryf-1 radar (starboard stern view).

Front boiler room area and right staircase to the forecastle. Starboard stern view.

Port side of the bow funnel base and front boiler room area.

The rear part of the forecastle.

Starboard side view of the bow PTA-53-30bis 533 mm torpedo launcher battery. The torpedo launcher is depicted in shooting position.

Starboard, front view of the mid superstructure with reserve ship control post.

Front part of mid superstructure. Port side, front view.

Port side view of mid superstructure towards stern.

Port side view of mid superstructure towards bow.

A rear view of the mid superstructure with stern funnel and two AA 70K gun 37mm.

Starboard side view of mid superstructure towards bow.

Starboard side view of mid superstructure towards stern.

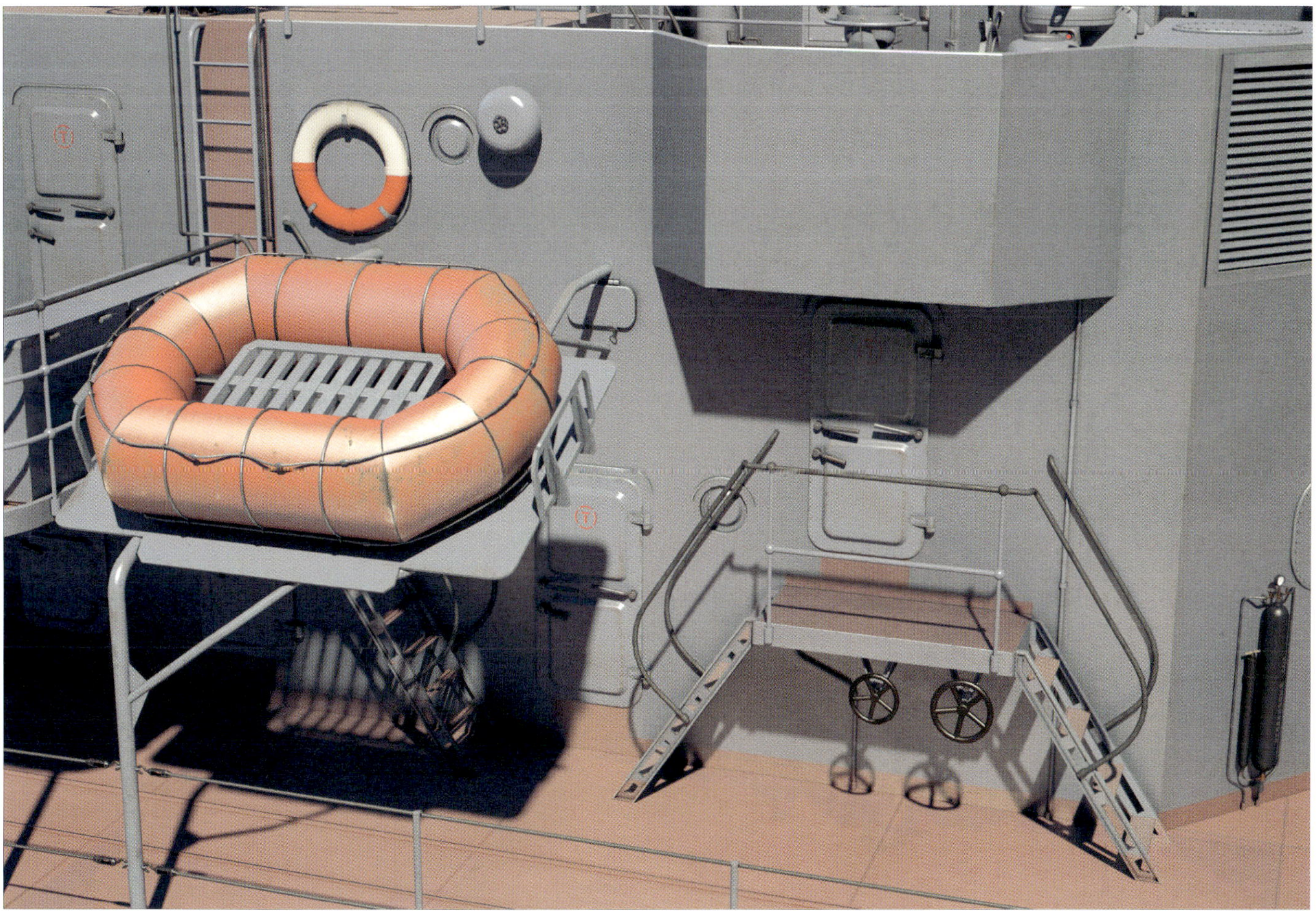

The rack with life raft of mid superstructure, starboard side.

Starboard AA 70K gun 37mm of the midships

AA 70K gun 37mm of the midships. Port stern view.

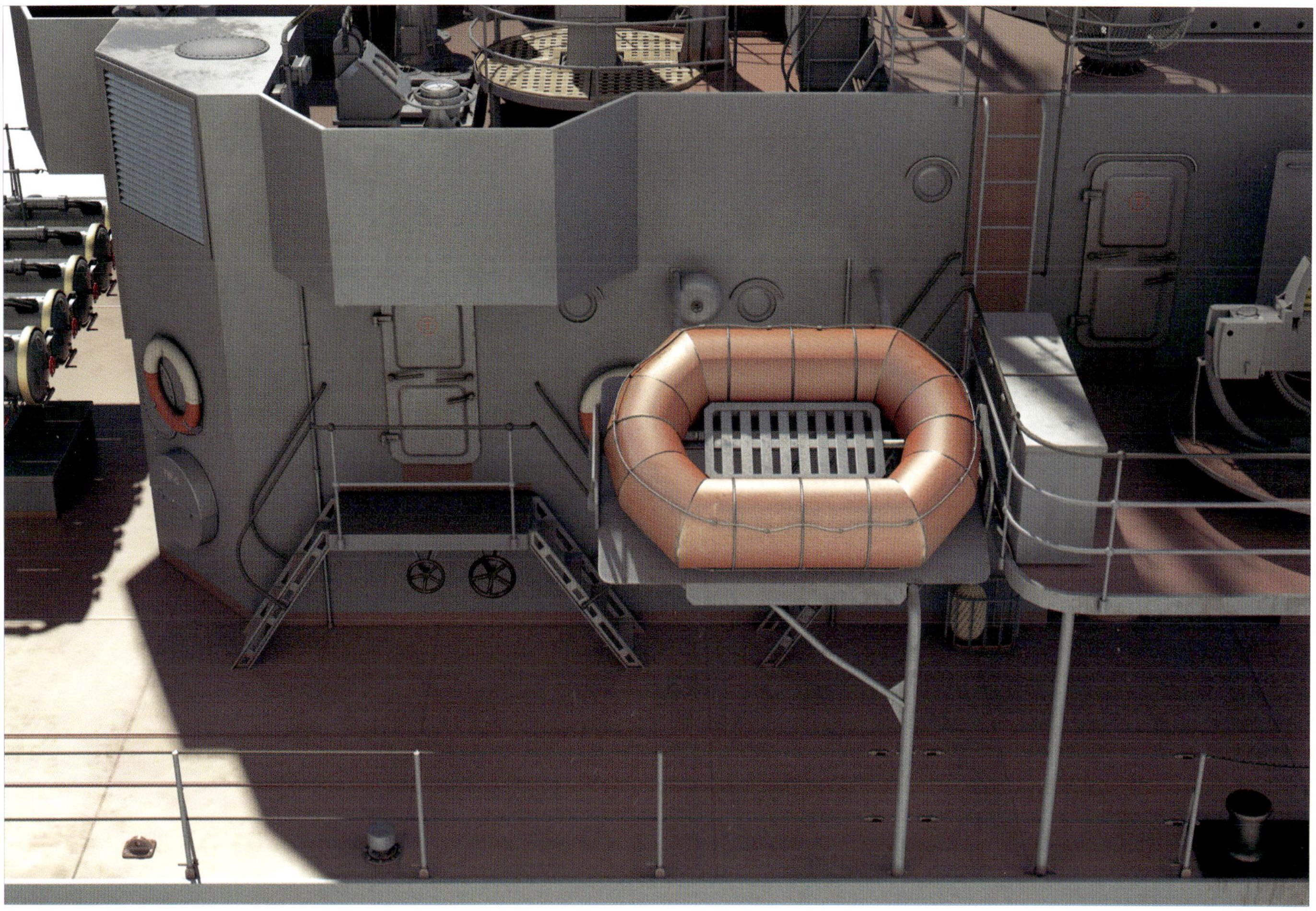

Port side of the midships superstructure and life raft.

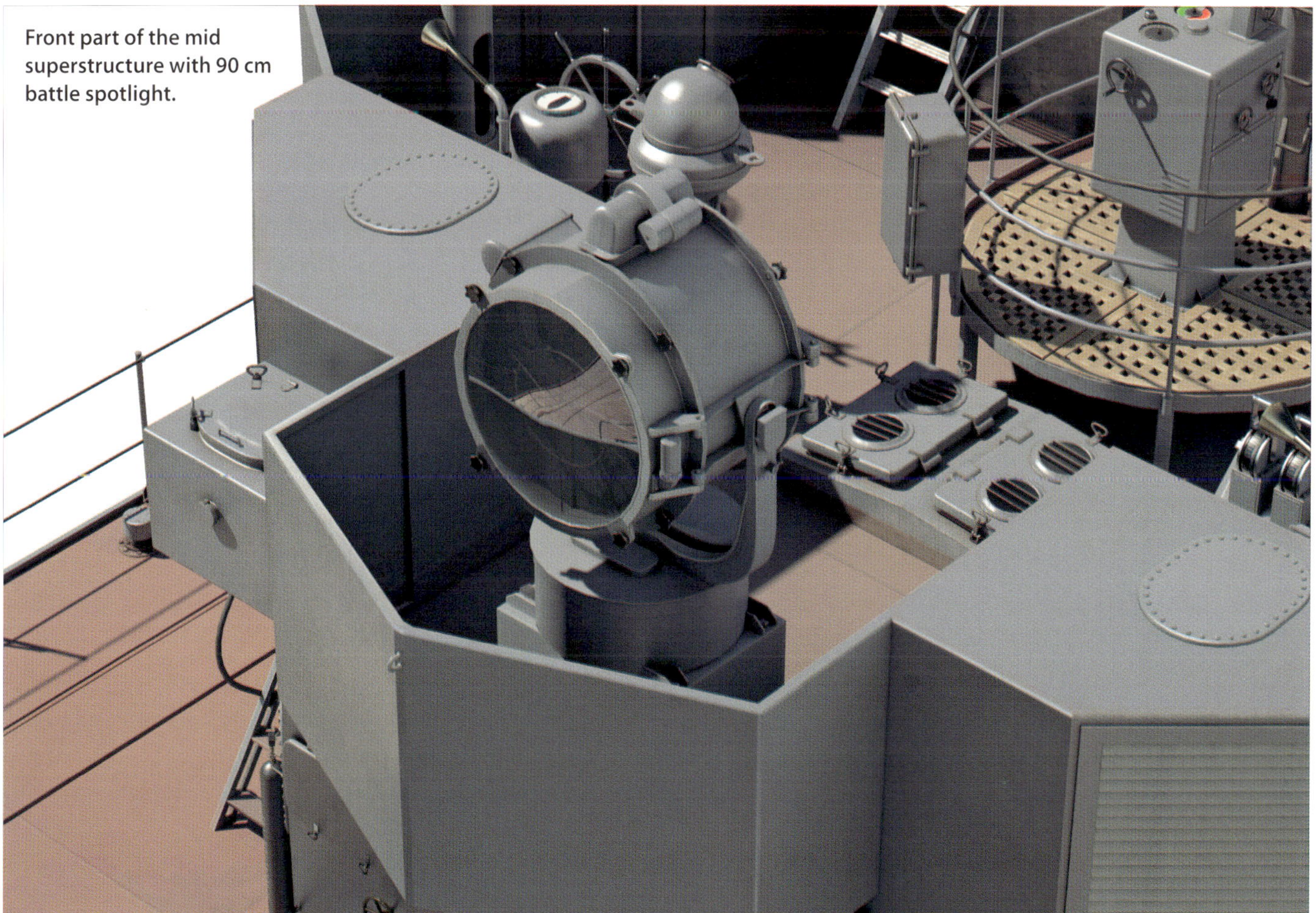

Front part of the mid superstructure with 90 cm battle spotlight.

Reserve ship control post.

12,7 mm 2m-1 mount and the aft funnel cover. Starboard bow view.

The aft funnel cover and 12,7 mm 2m-1 mount. Starboard stern view.

Port side view of the 12,7 mm 2m-1 mount and the aft funnel cover.

12,7 mm 2m-1 mount , the aft funnel cover and surrounding details. Port bow view.

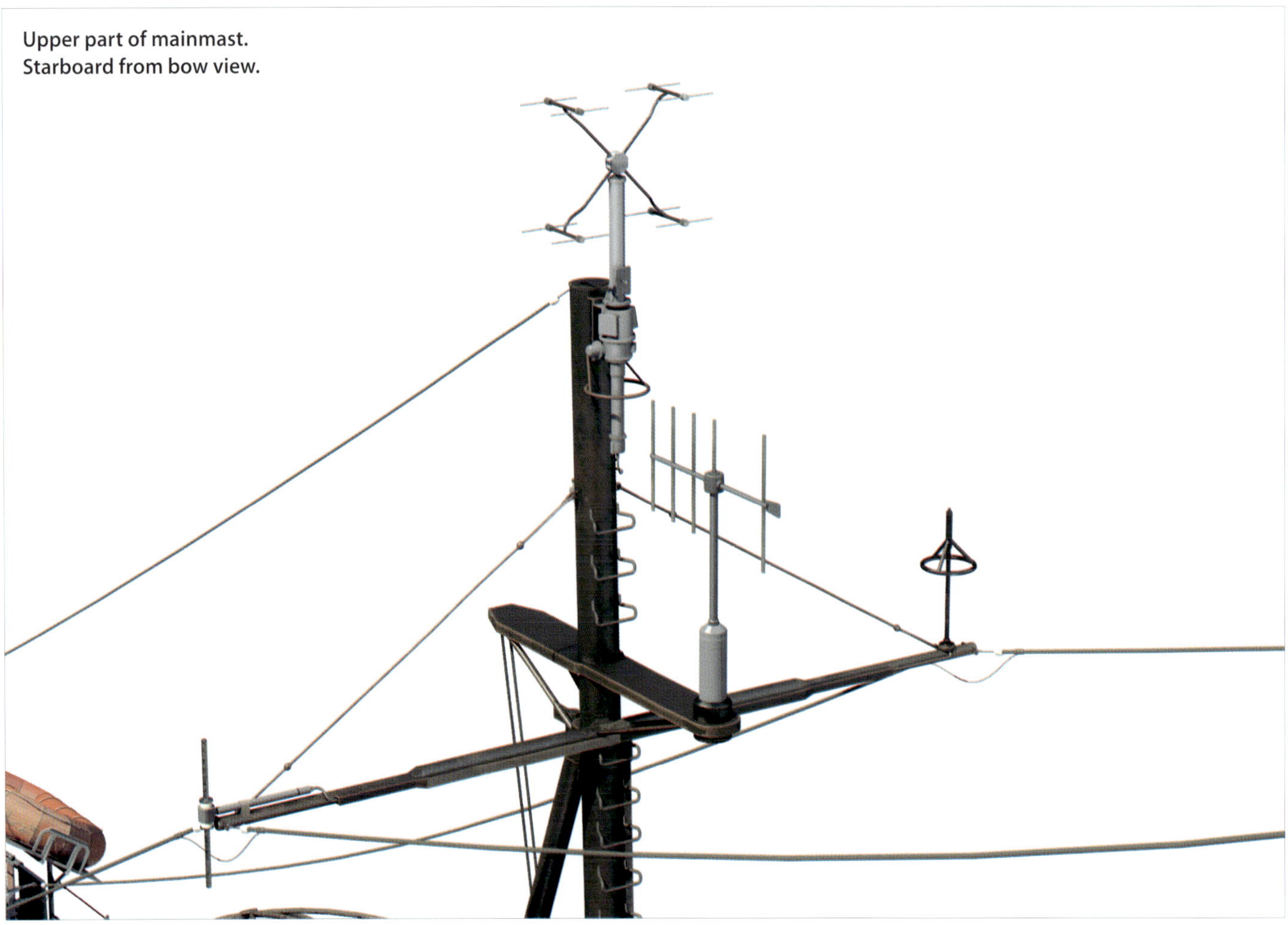

Upper part of mainmast.
Starboard from bow view.

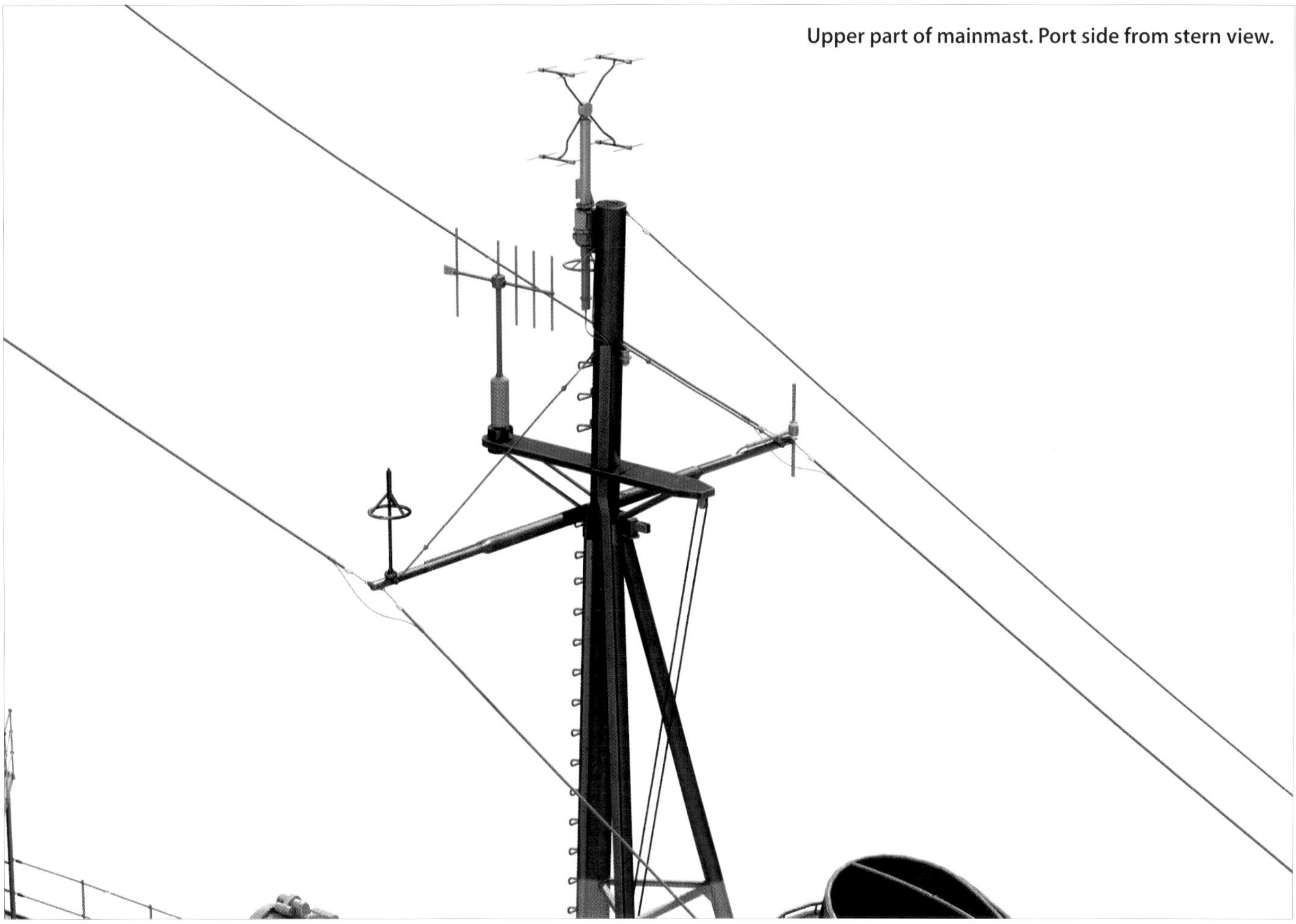
Upper part of mainmast. Port side from stern view.

Gyus-1 radar mounted on top of the mainmast. Starboard from bow view.

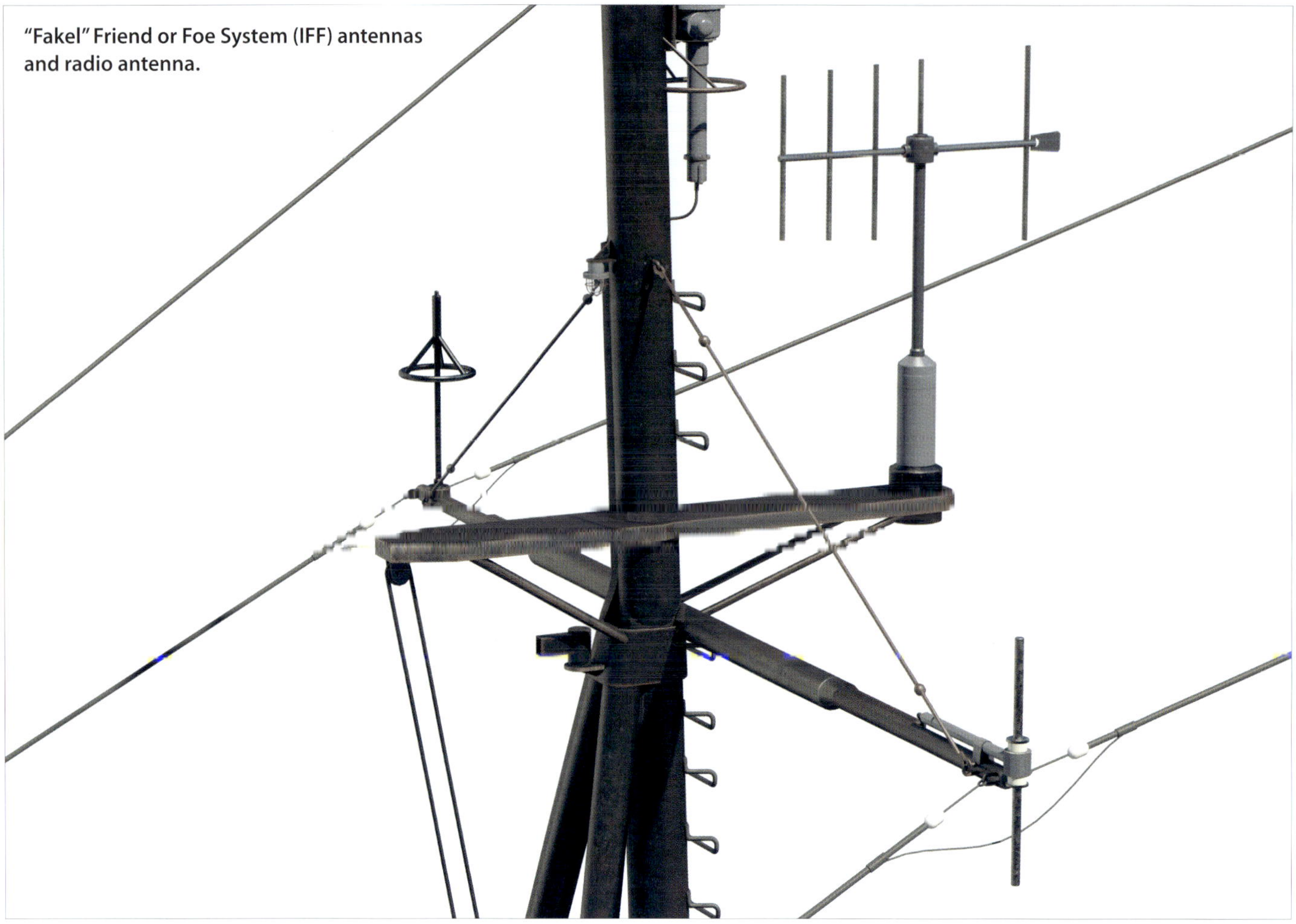
"Fakel" Friend or Foe System (IFF) antennas and radio antenna.

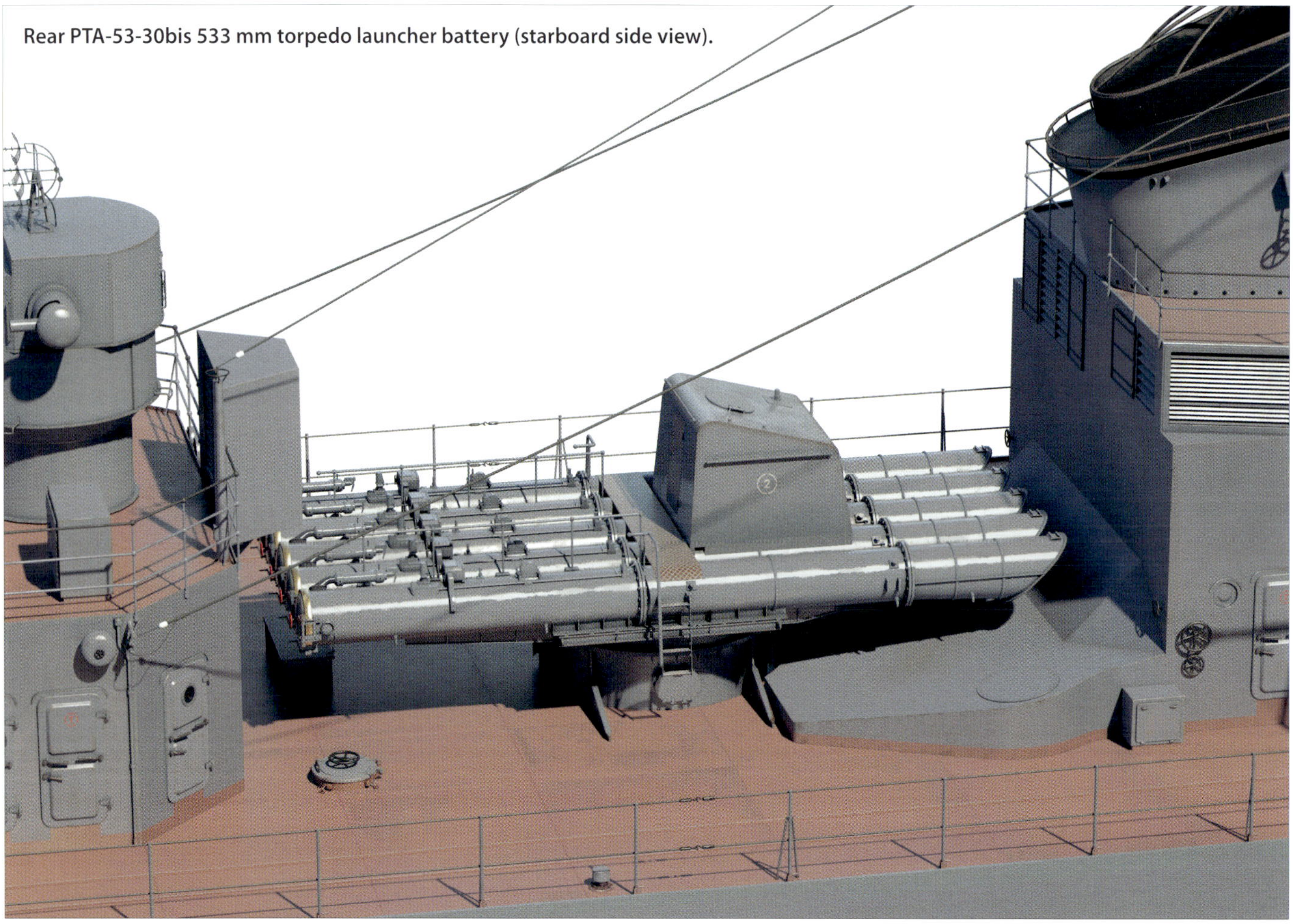
Rear PTA-53-30bis 533 mm torpedo launcher battery (starboard side view).

The same rear PTA-53-30bis 533 mm torpedo launcher (port side view).

Port side view of rear PTA-53-30bis 533 mm torpedo launcher in shooting position.

Port side view of the stern superstructure.

Front part of the stern superstructure (port bow view).

Front part of the stern superstructure (starboard view).

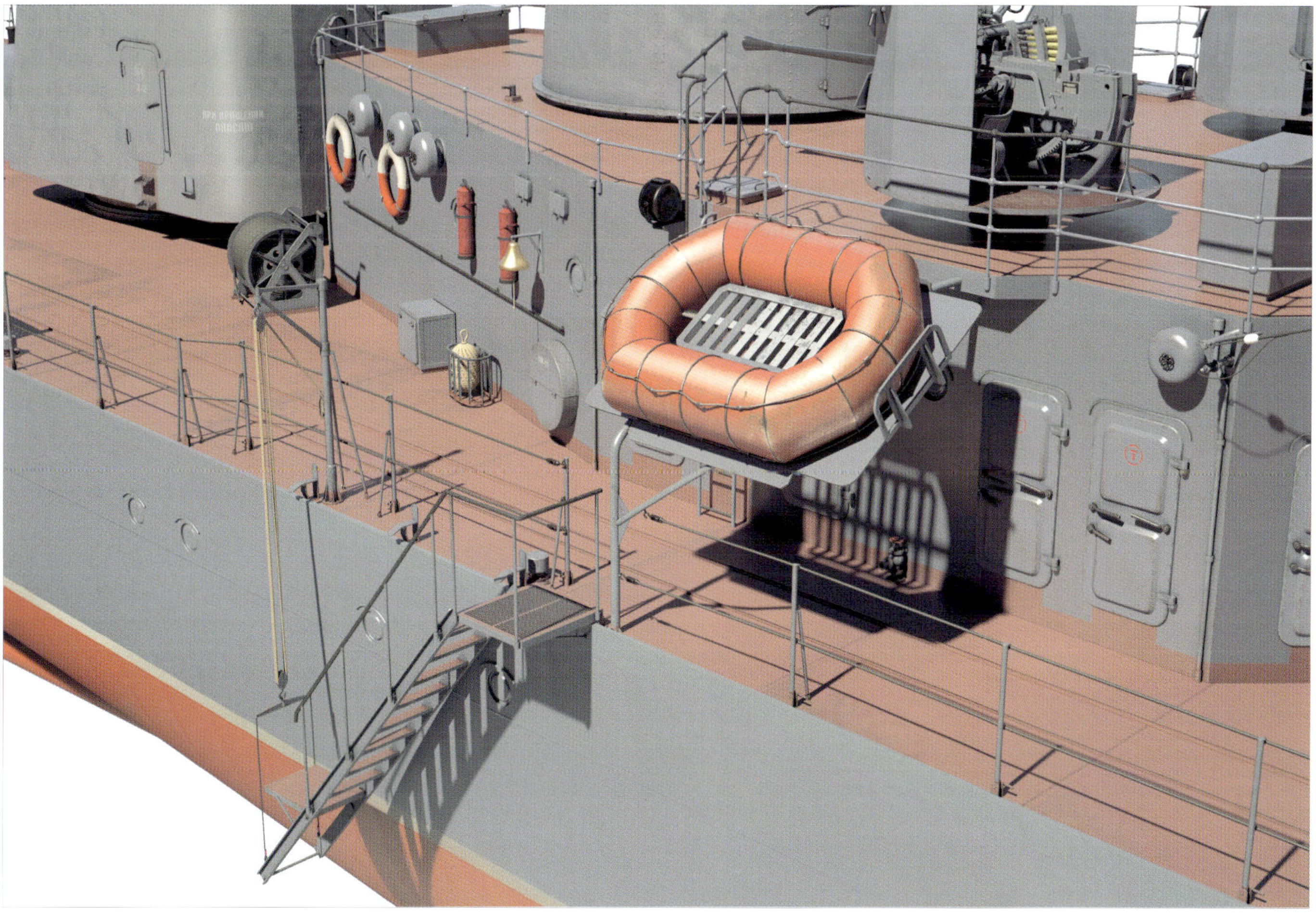

Starboard view of the stern superstructure mid part and unfolded starboard ladder.

Another starboard view of the stern superstructure mid part.

Rear part of the stern superstructure (starboard view).

Rear part of the stern superstructure (port view).

Rear part of the stern superstructure (port view).

Folded port side ladder.

Port side view area of the stern superstructure.

Two 37mm AA 70 K of the stern superstructure.

SVP-29RLM stabilized optical post with "Vympel-2"artillery radar.

SVP-29RLM stabilized optical post with "Vympel-2"artillery radar.

85mm 92K universal turret. (starboard bow view).

Starboard stern view of the 85mm 92K turret.

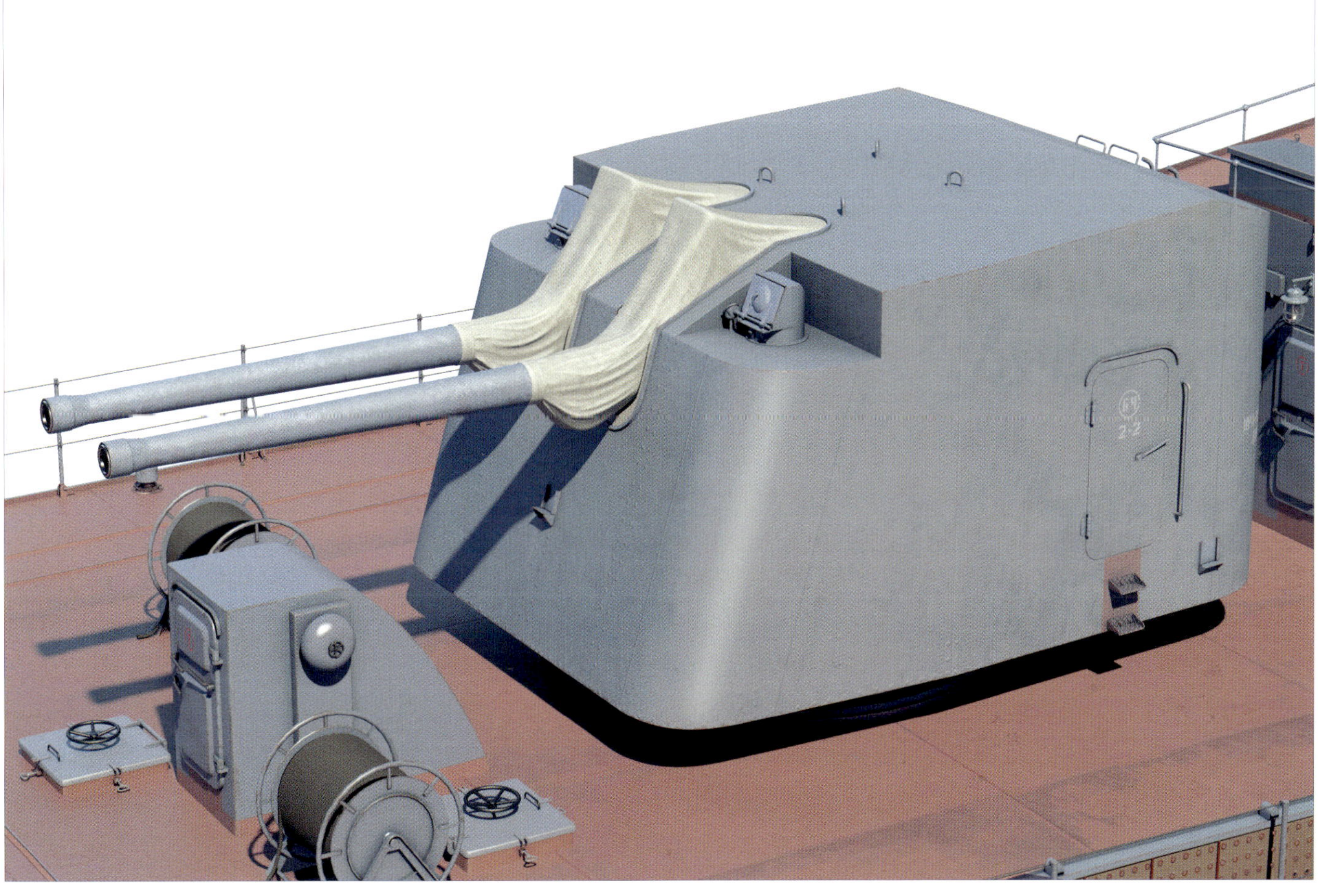

Starboard side view of the stern 130mm B-2 LM main artillery turret.

Stern 130mm B-2 LM main artillery turret. In front of the turret is a stairwell.

Stern deck with a two stairwells and depth charge devices.

Two BMB-1 depth charge throwers and depth charge racks (port stern view).

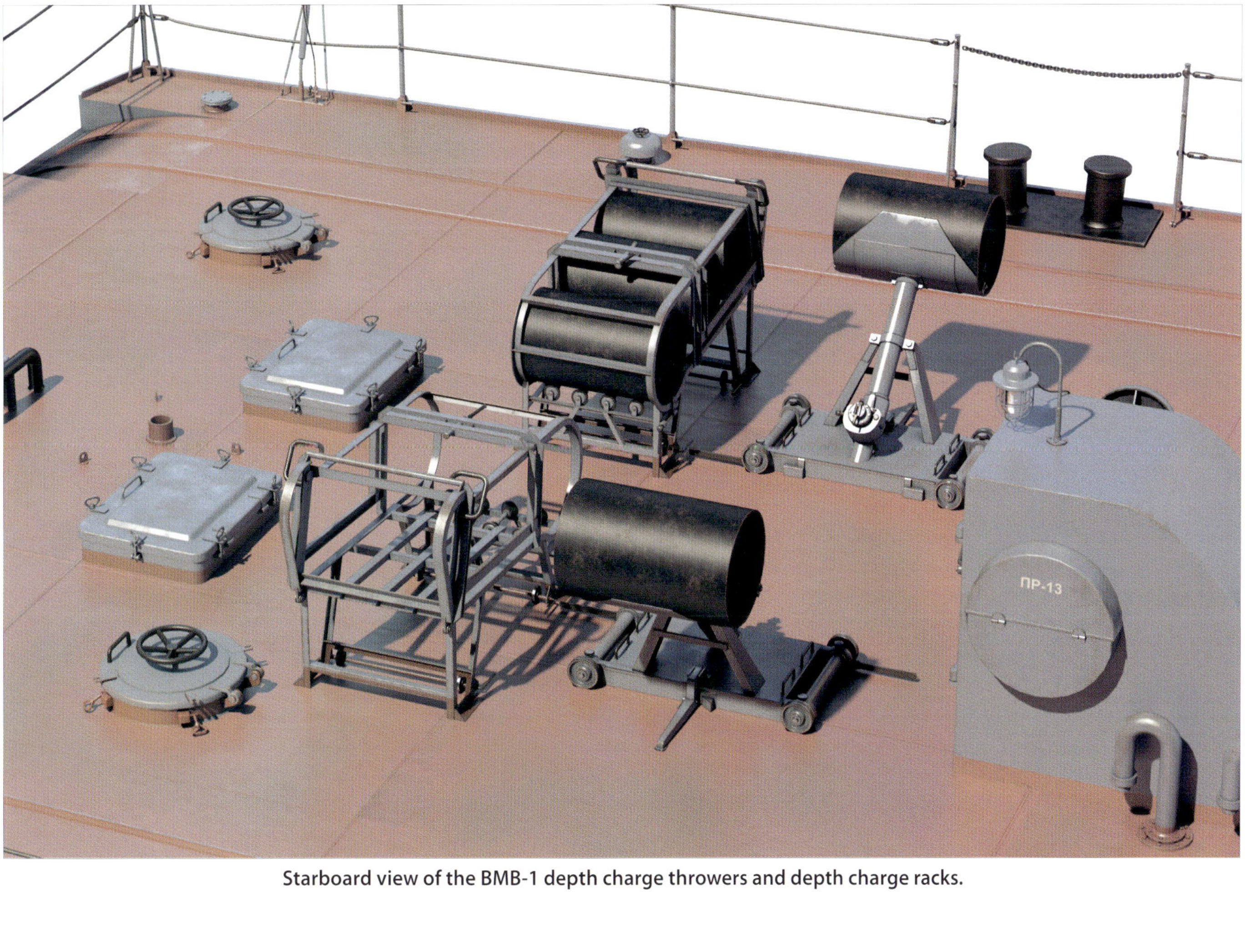

Starboard view of the BMB-1 depth charge throwers and depth charge racks.

Left, not loaded depth charge racks (stern view).

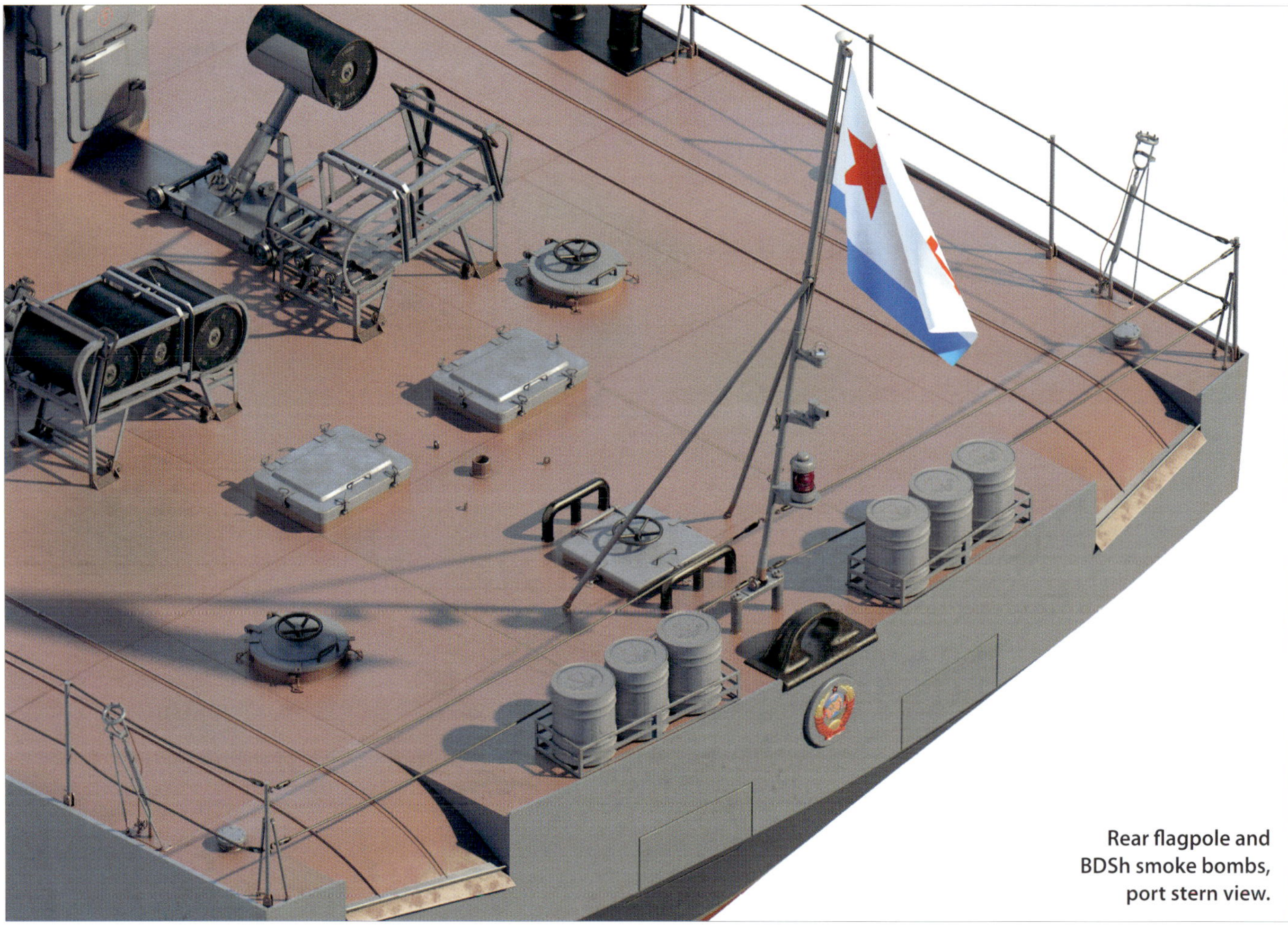
Rear flagpole and BDSh smoke bombs, port stern view.

Left nozzle smoke equipment, port view.

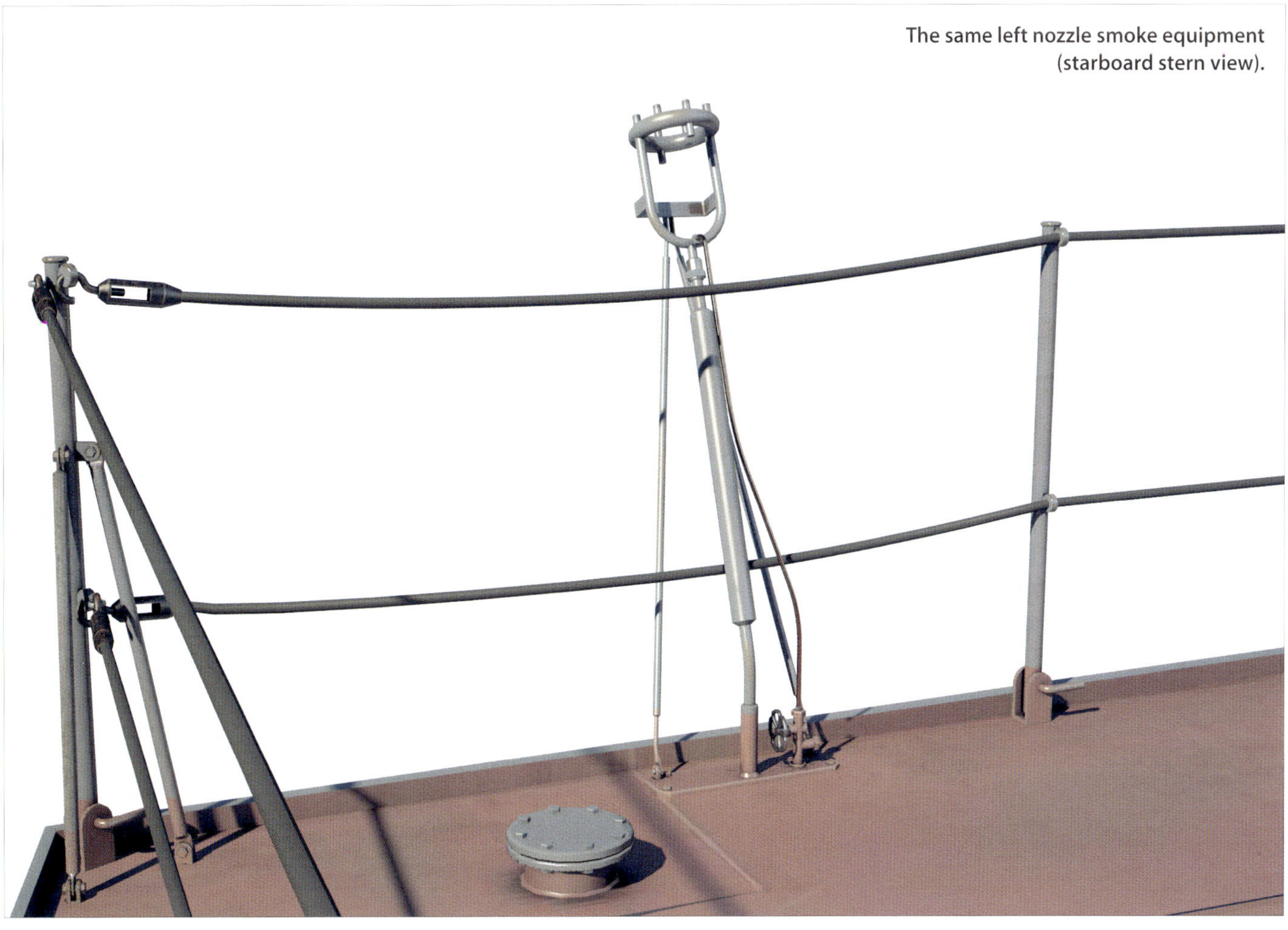

The same left nozzle smoke equipment (starboard stern view).

BDSh smoke bombs.

Port view of the rear flagpole details.

The stern of the ship.

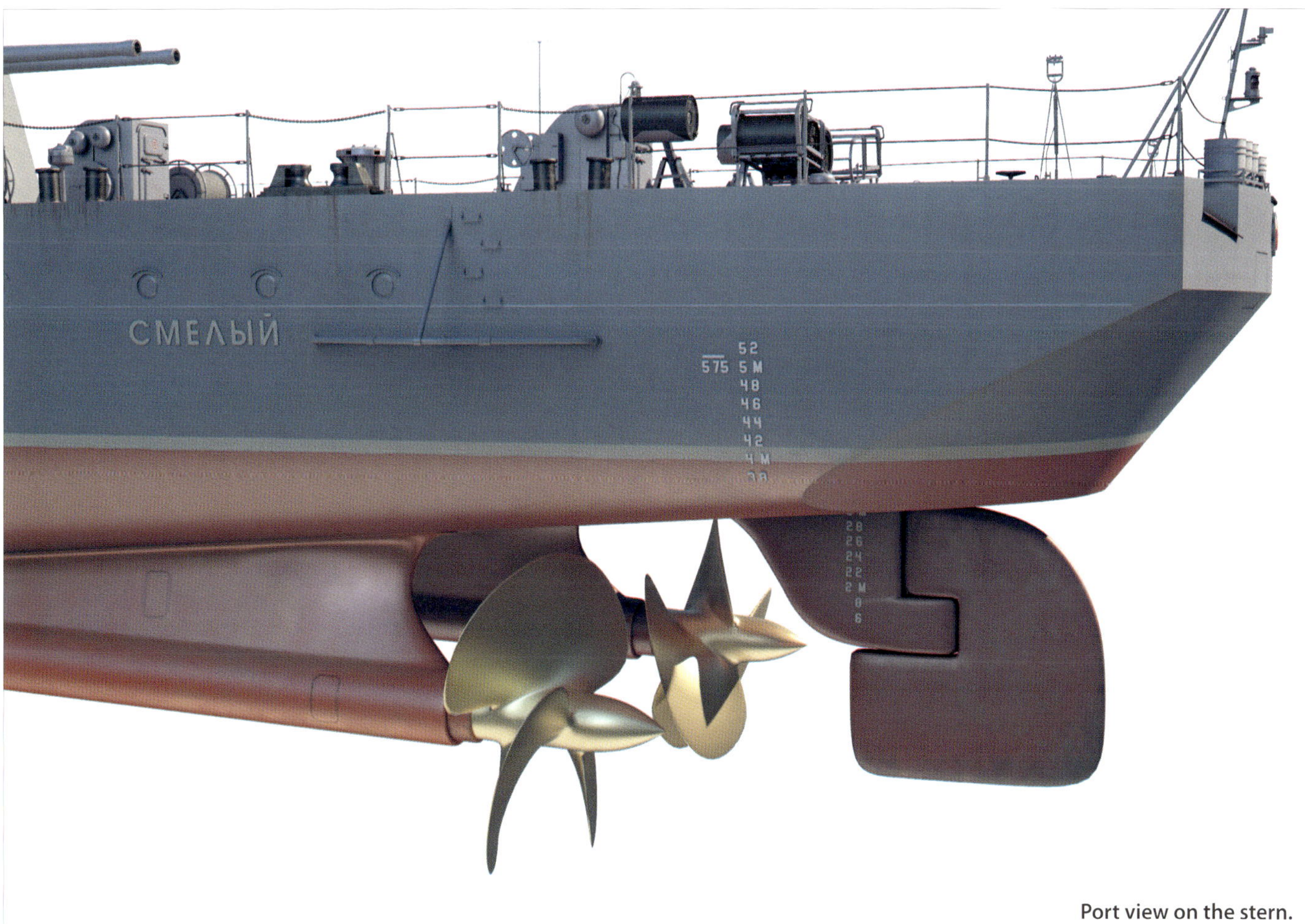

Port view on the stern.

The mine B-2LM turret.

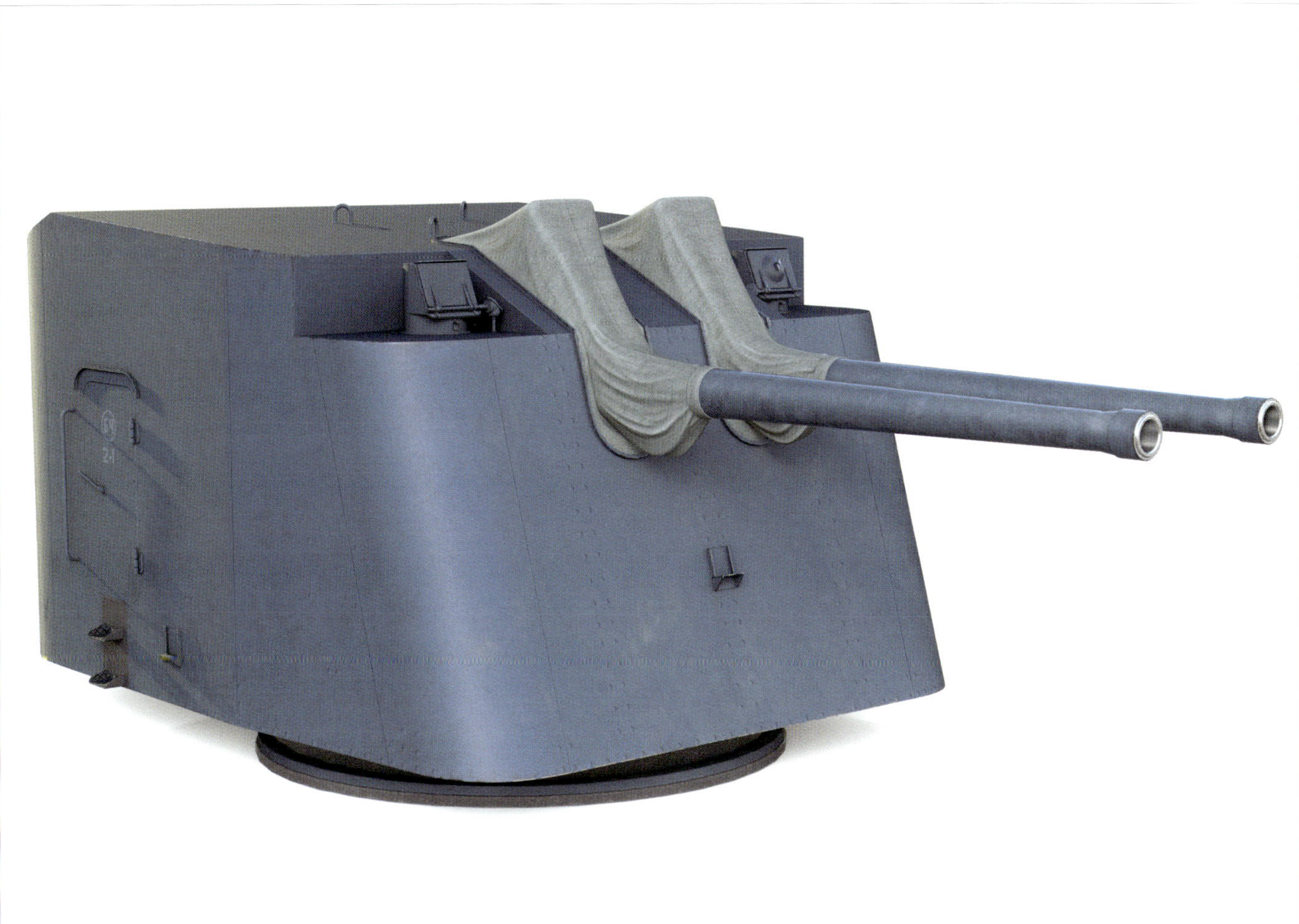

The twin universal 92K 85mm gun mount.

The twin universal 92K turret n position for shooting air targets.

37mm AA 70K gun.

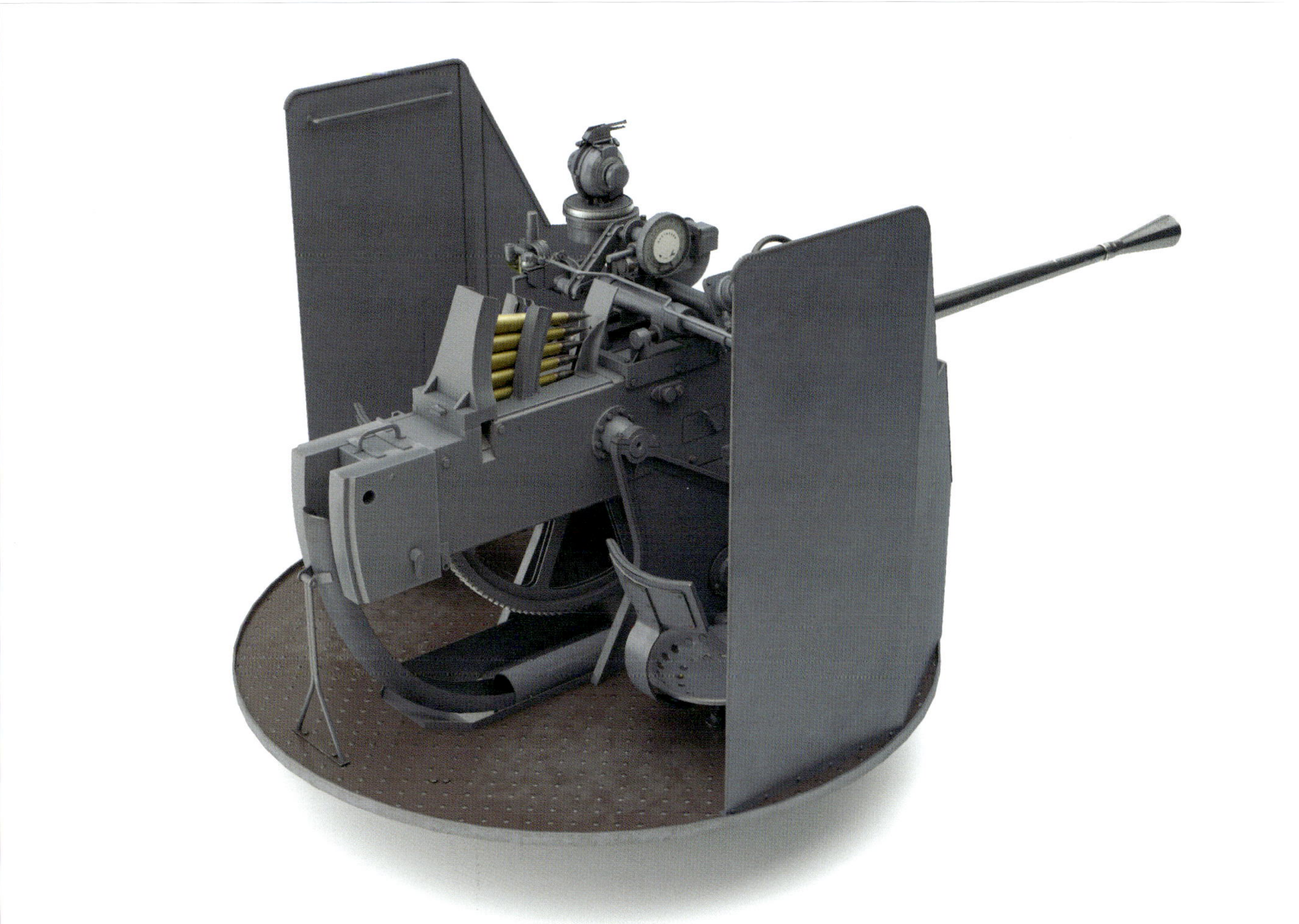

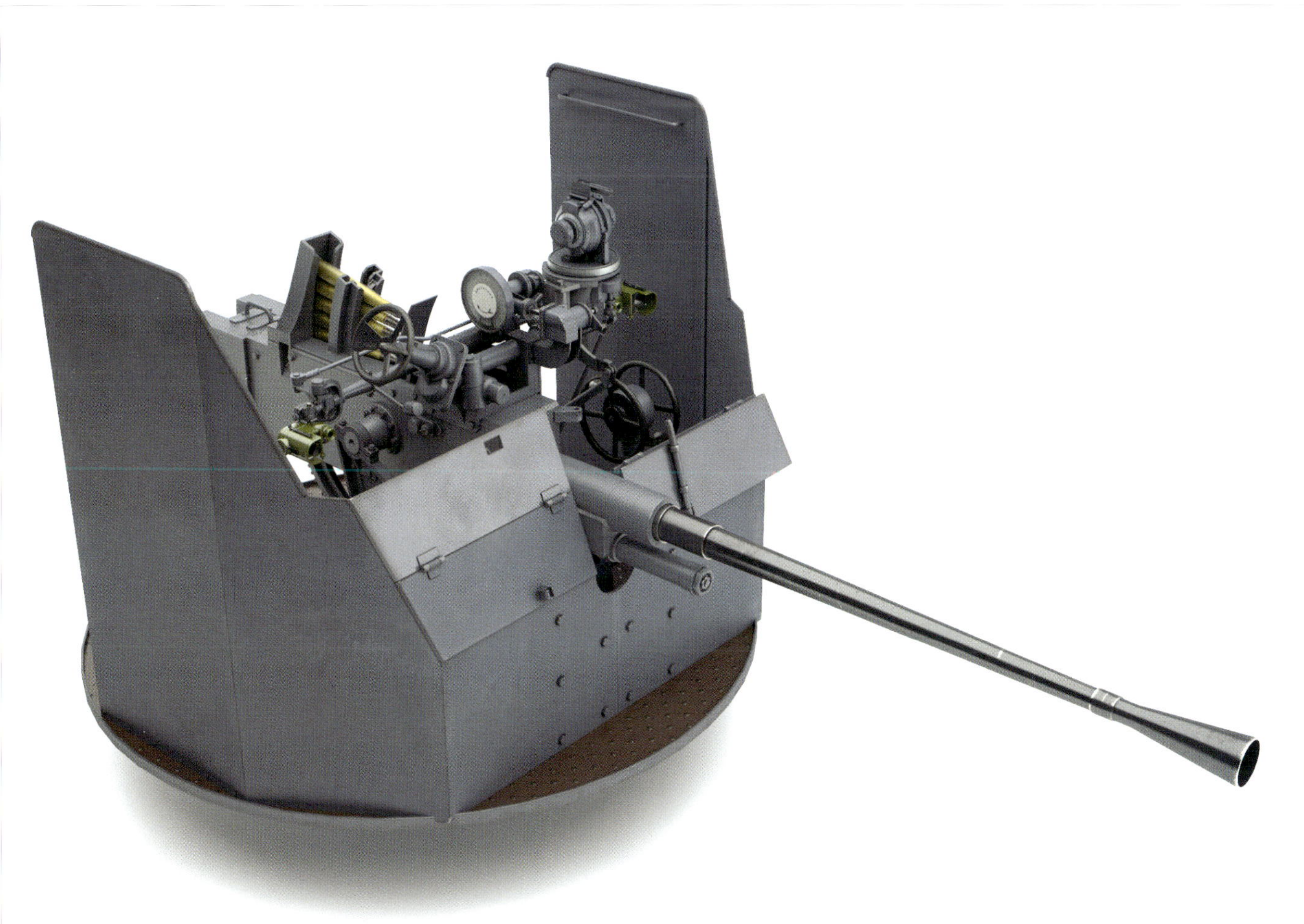

37mm AA 70K gun without armor plates.

The left part of the sight, which serves to set the angles of diving and cabling. Back view.

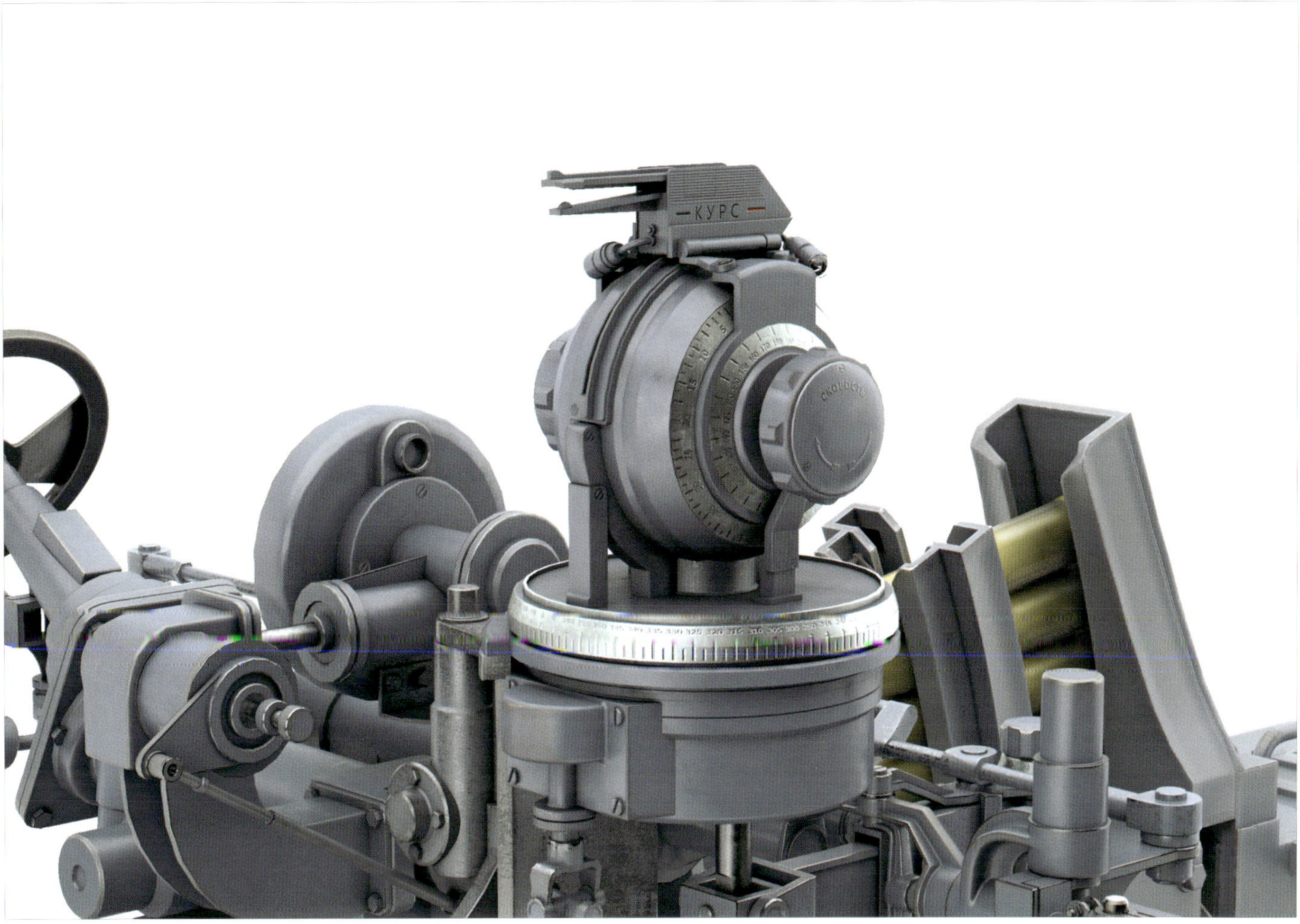

The right part of the sight, which serves to set the speed of target and distance. Right side view.

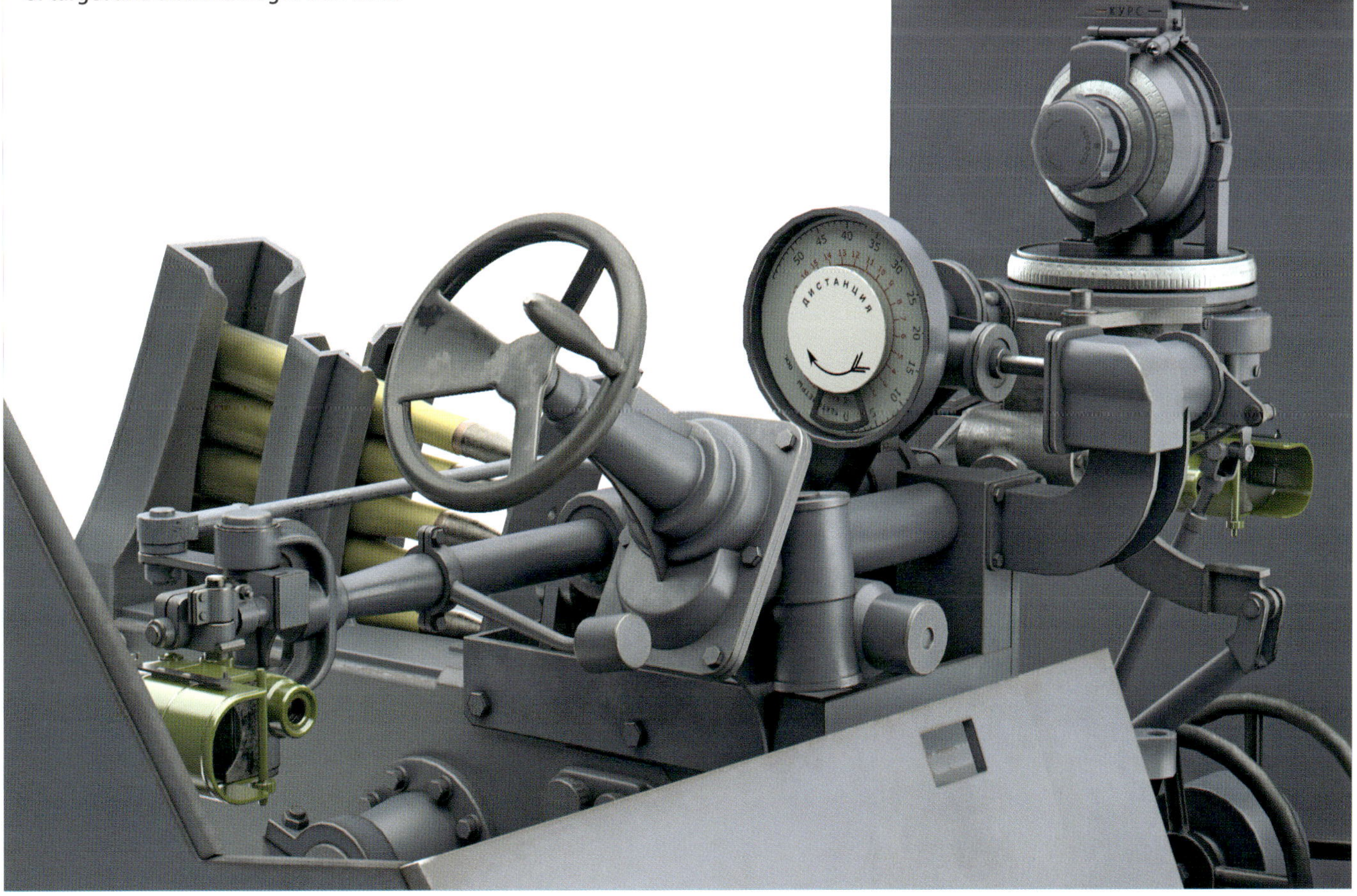

PTA-53-30bis 533 mm torpedo launcher battery.

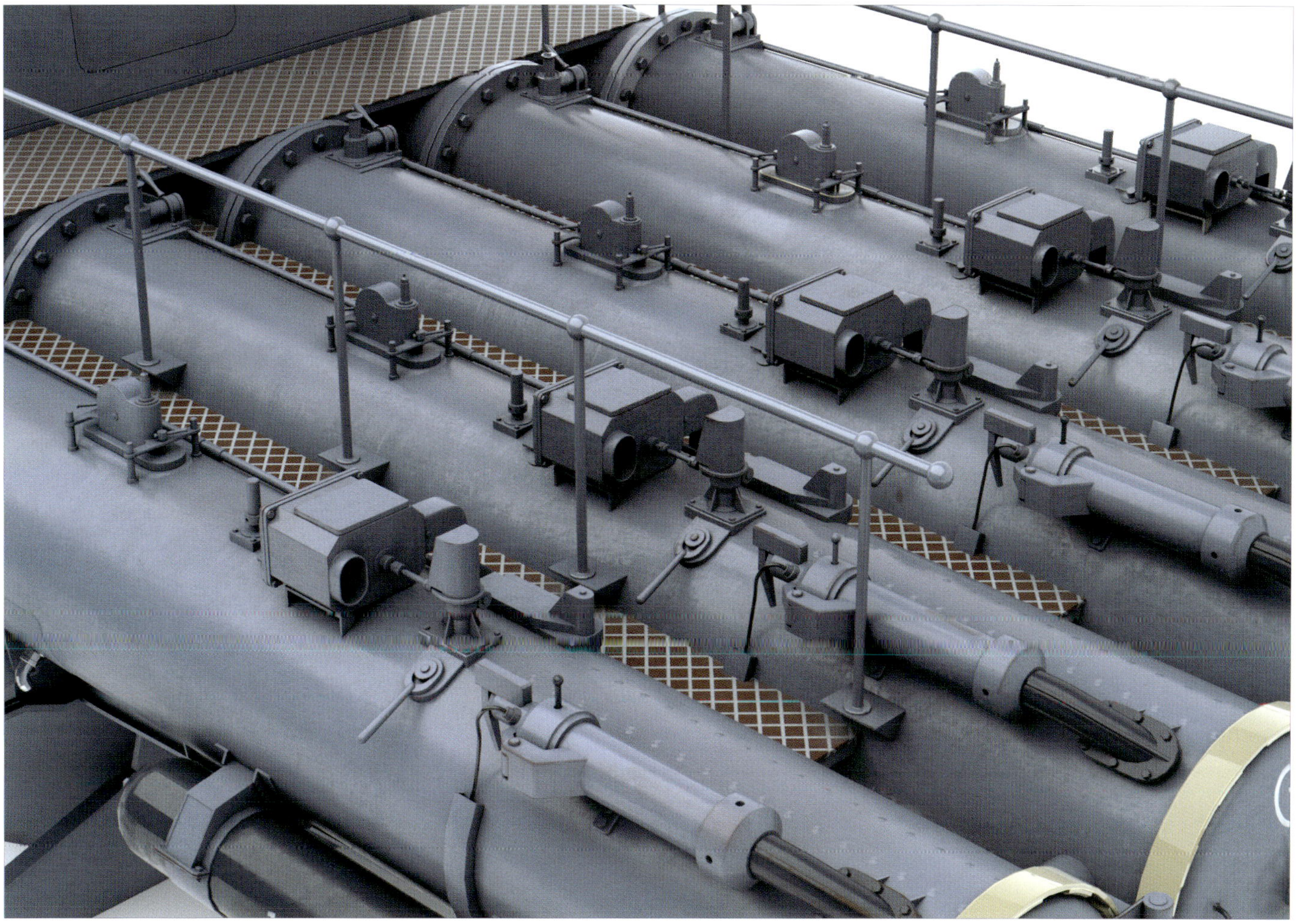

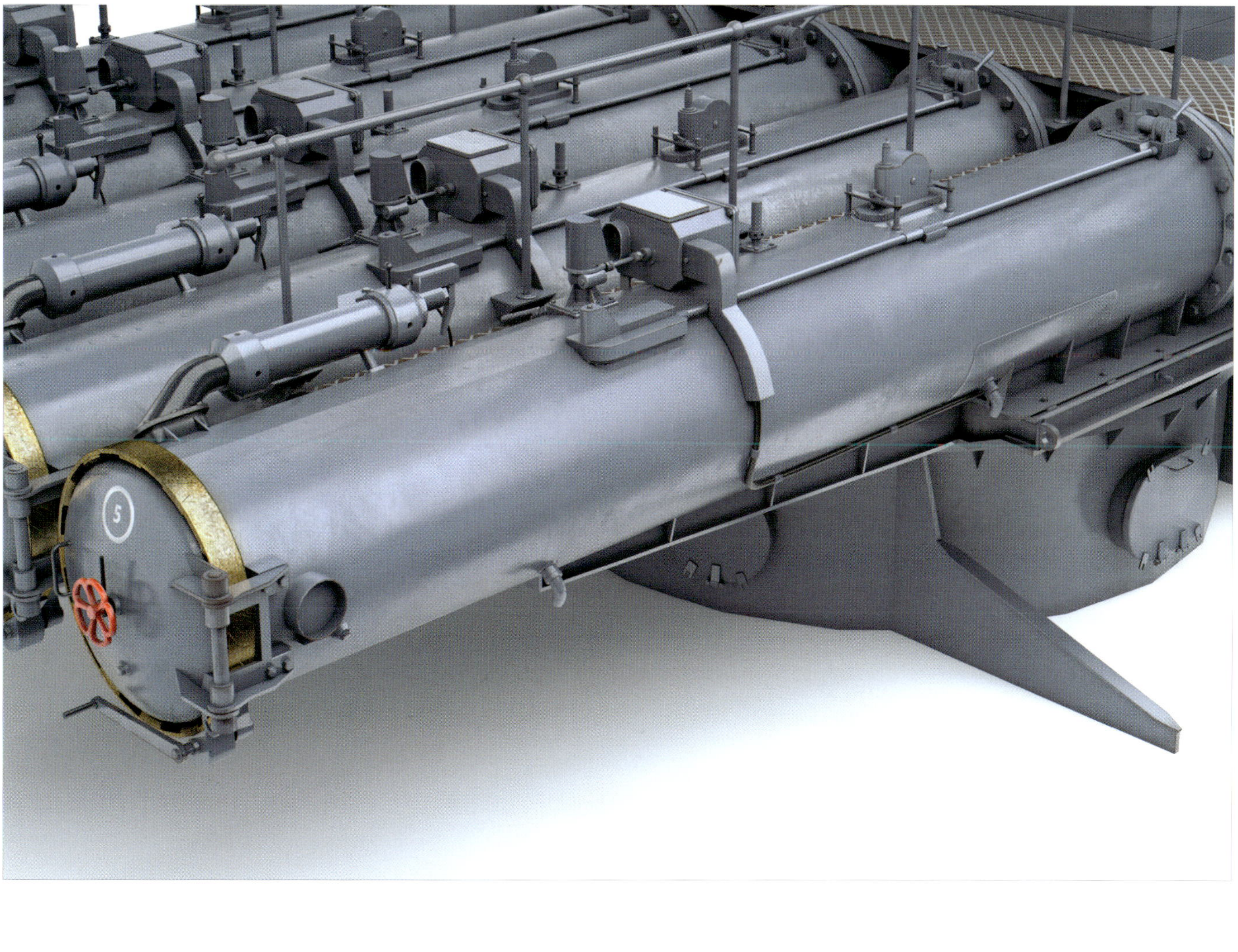

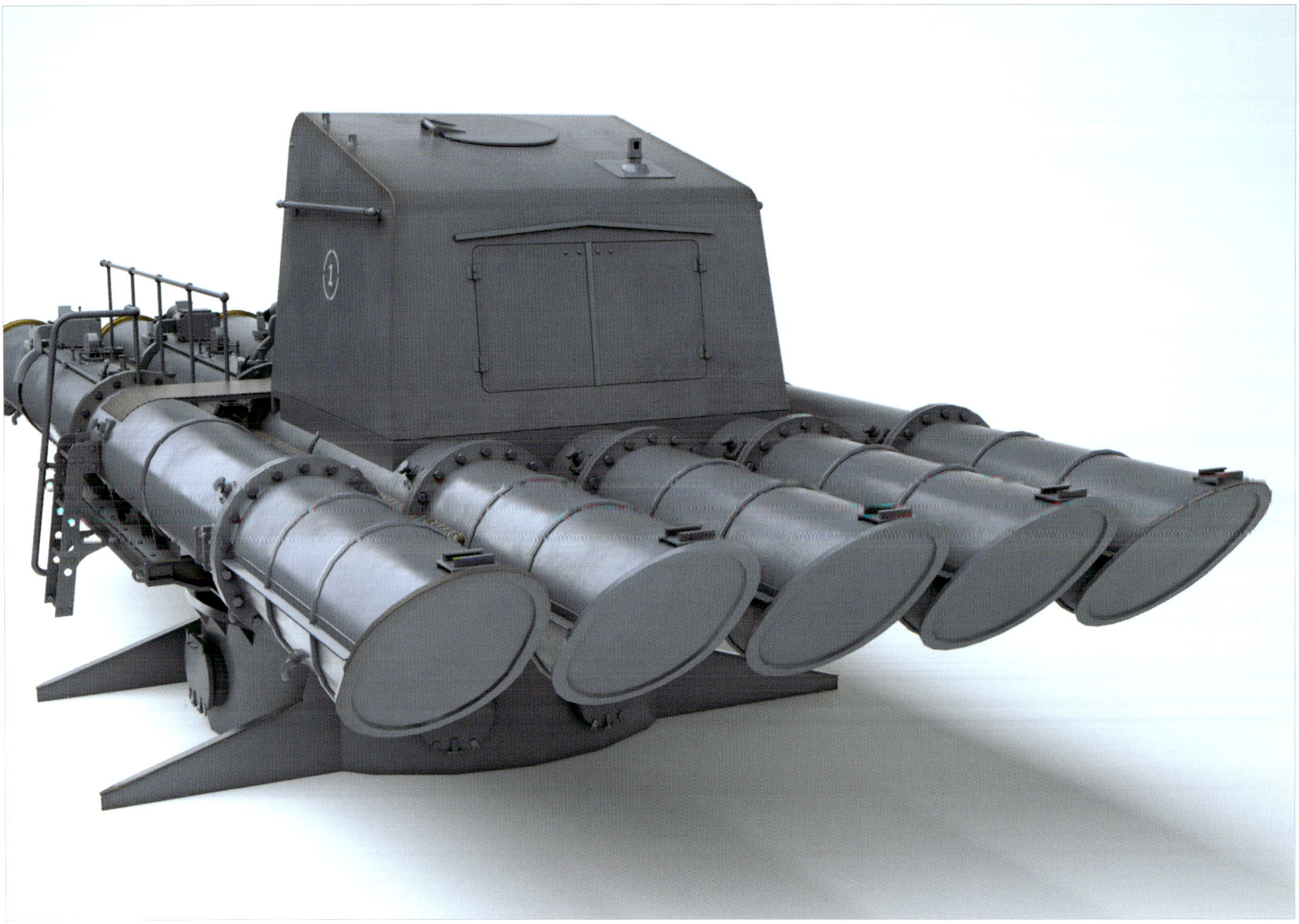

Commander's motor boat proj. 378.

Work cutter proj.386.

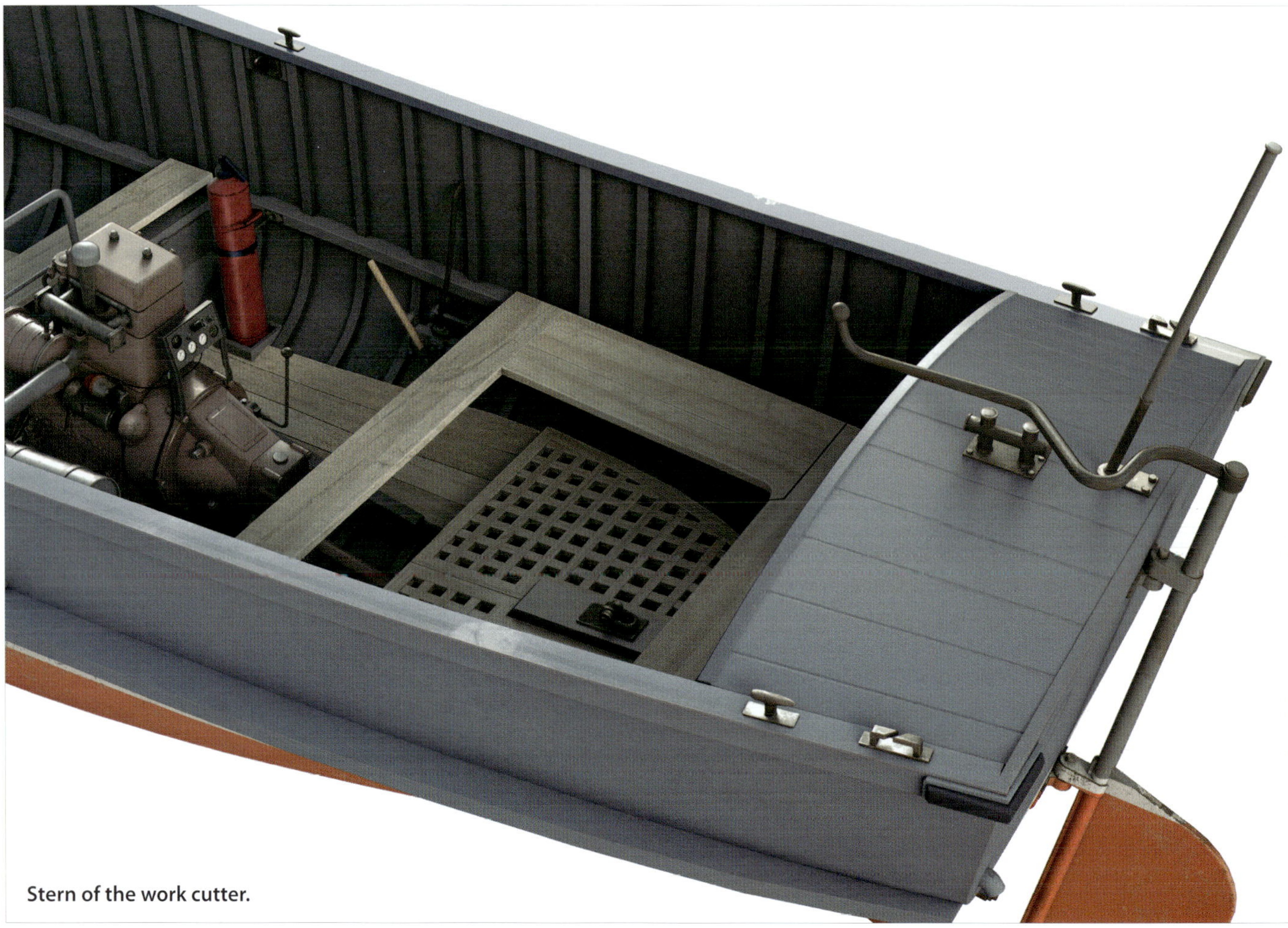

Stern of the work cutter.

Details of the work cutter.

Bow details of work cutter. Stern view.

Six- oared yal type 6.

The same yal seen from the bow side.

BMB depth charge thrower with BB-1 depth charge.

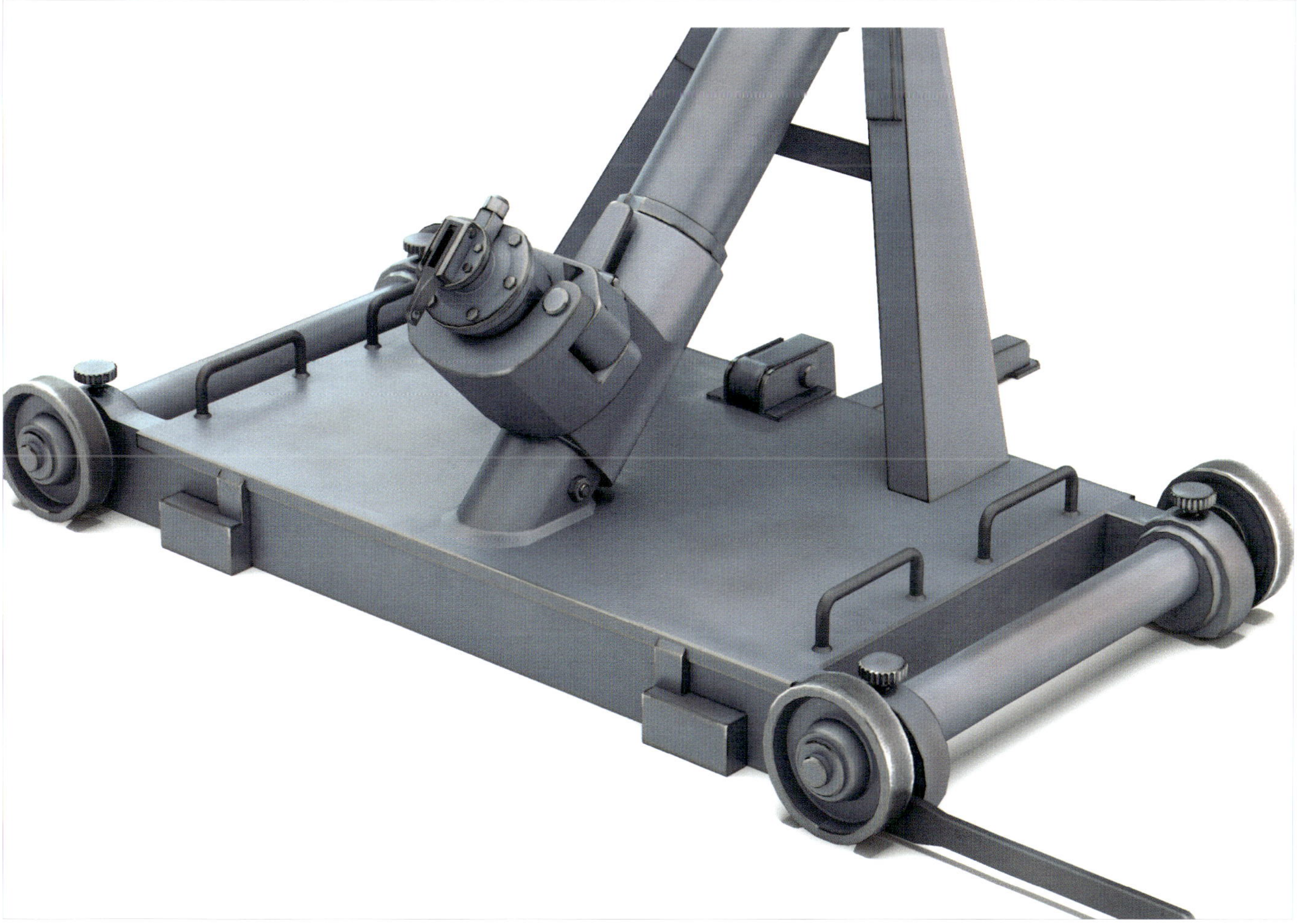

VCUZ-1

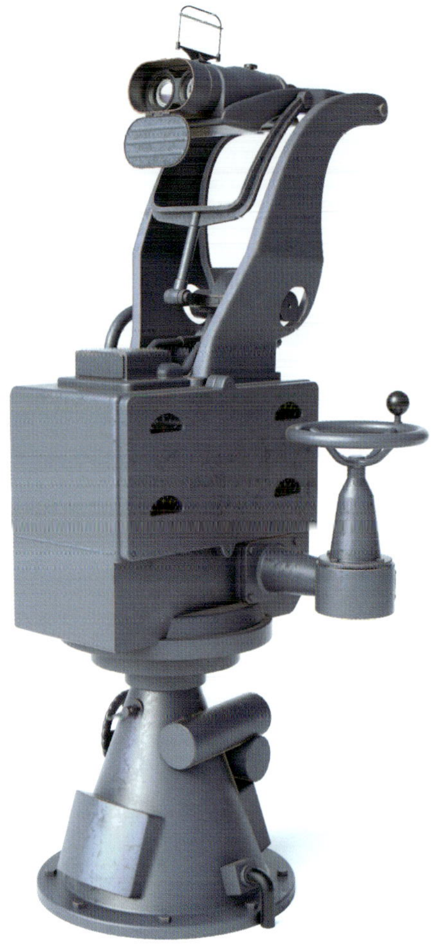

Binocular optical device of VCUZ-1.

MPE-E 9.0 90 cm battle spotlight. Front view.

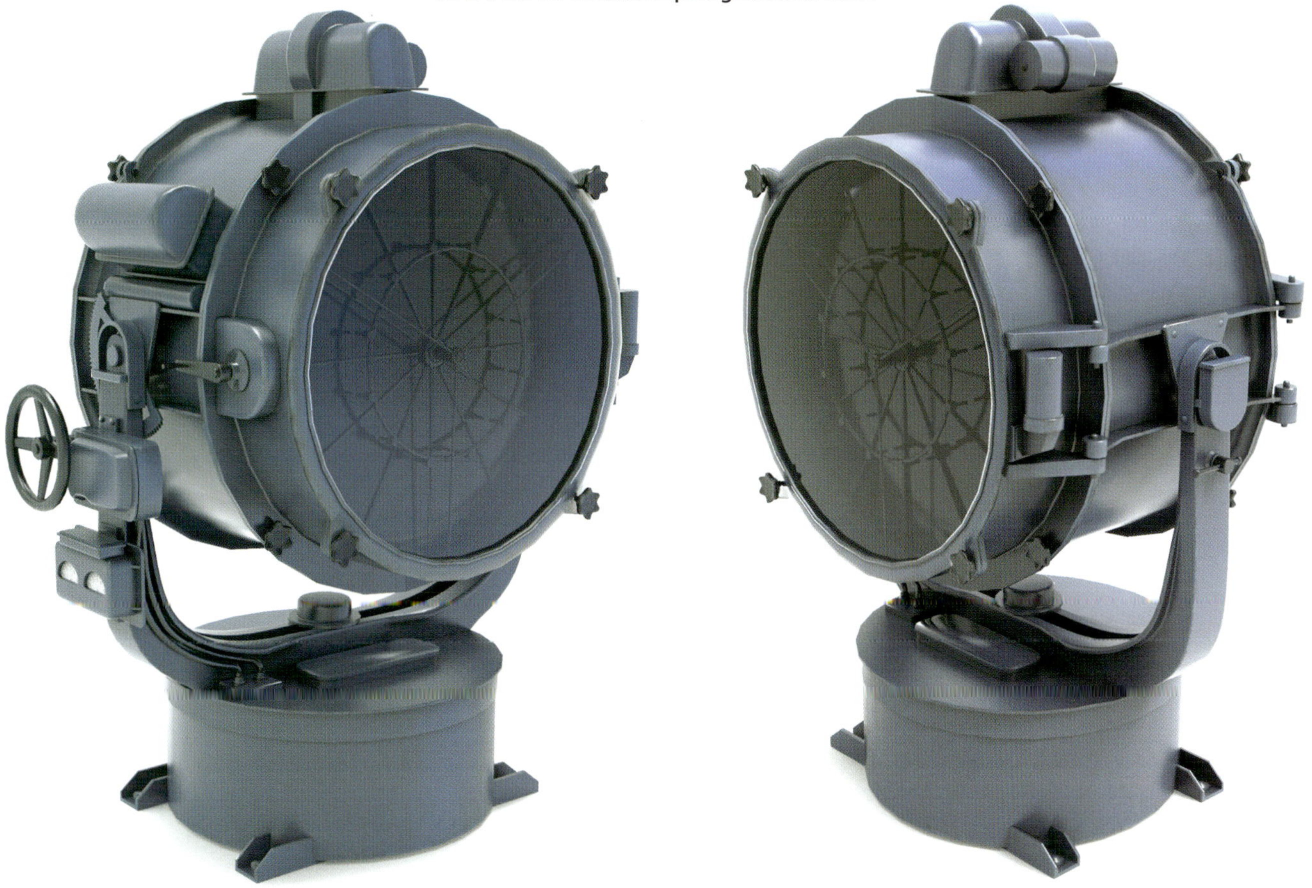

MPE-E 9.0 90 cm battle spotlight. Back view.

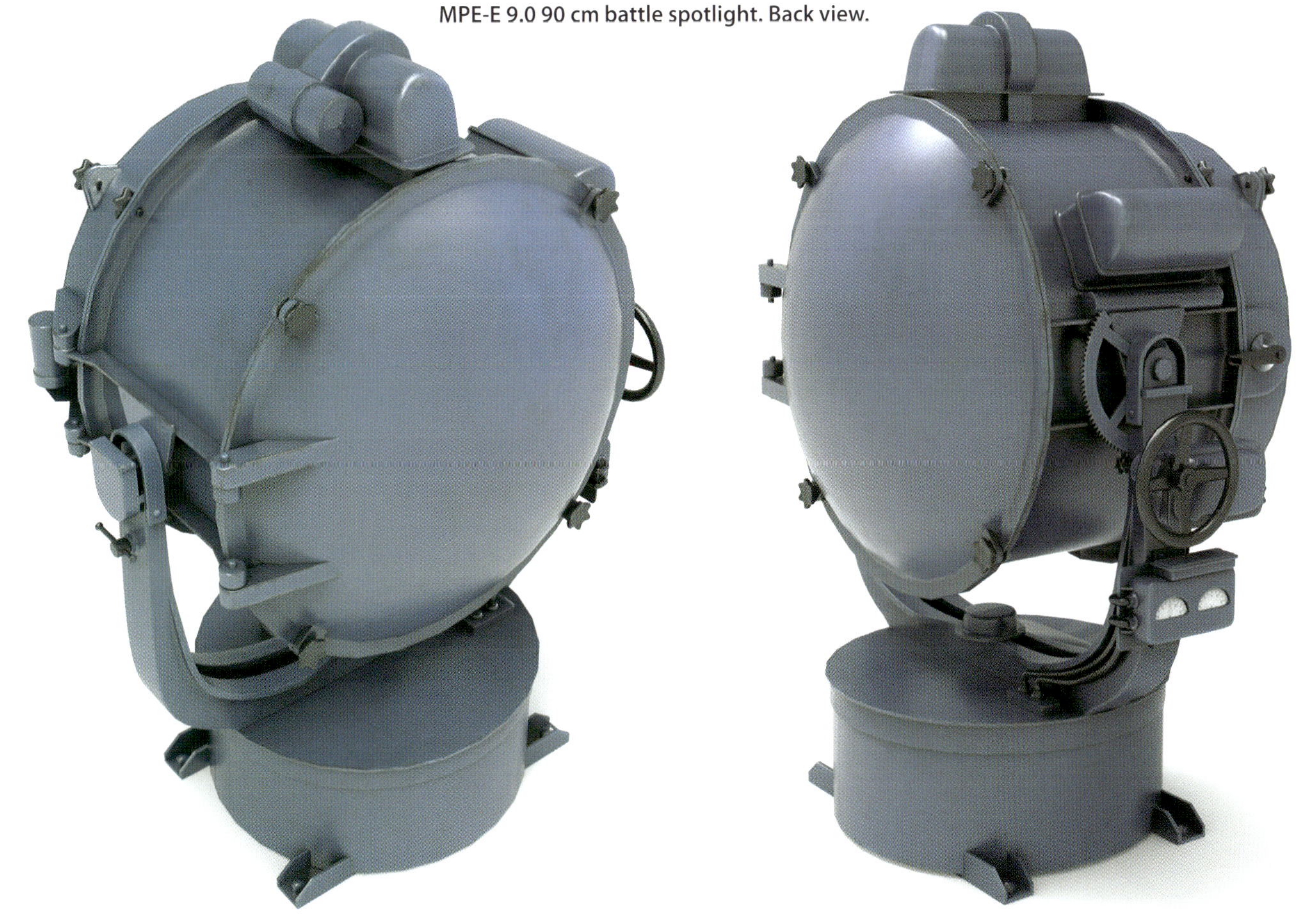

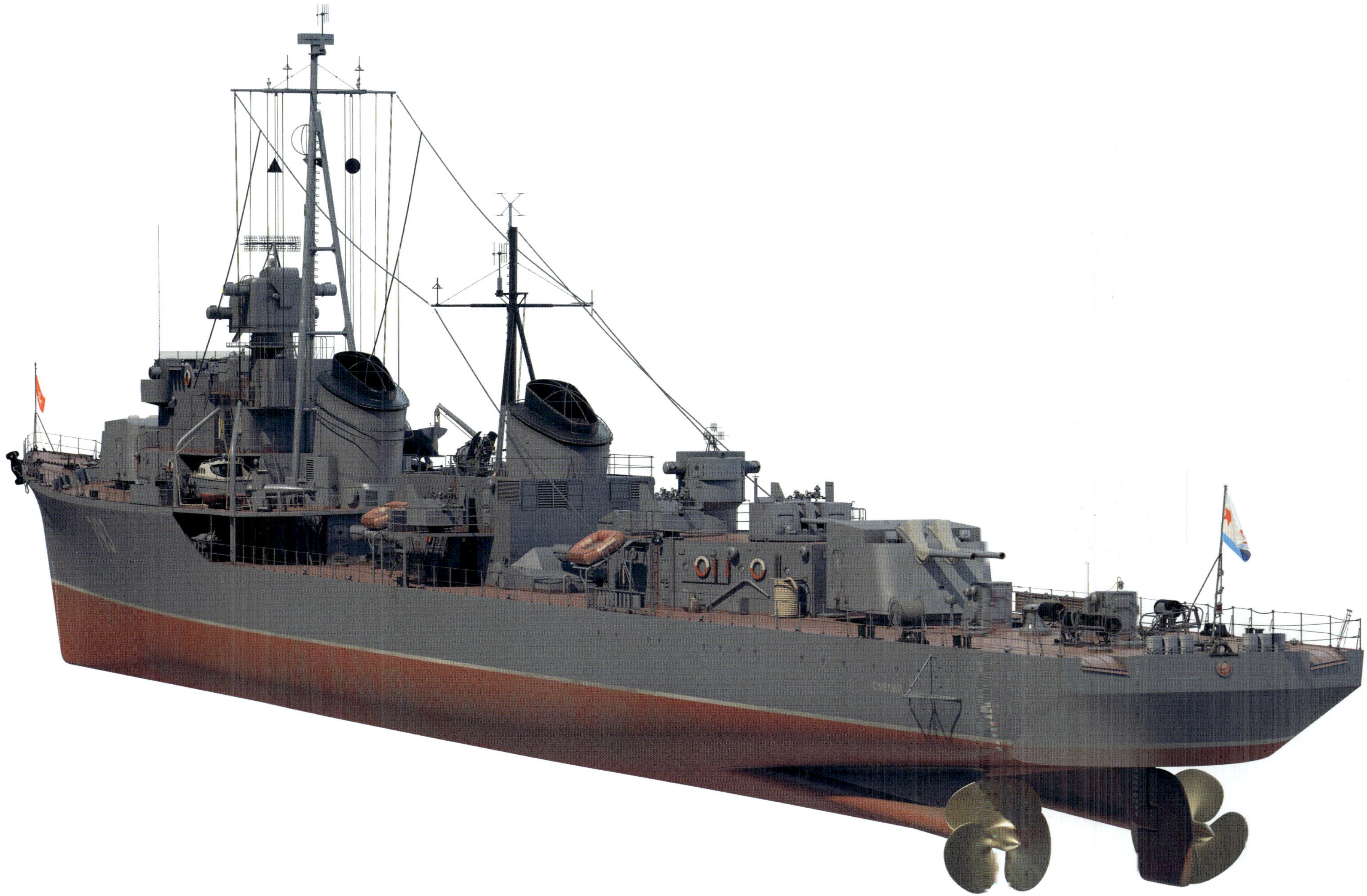

View of the ship from the stern.

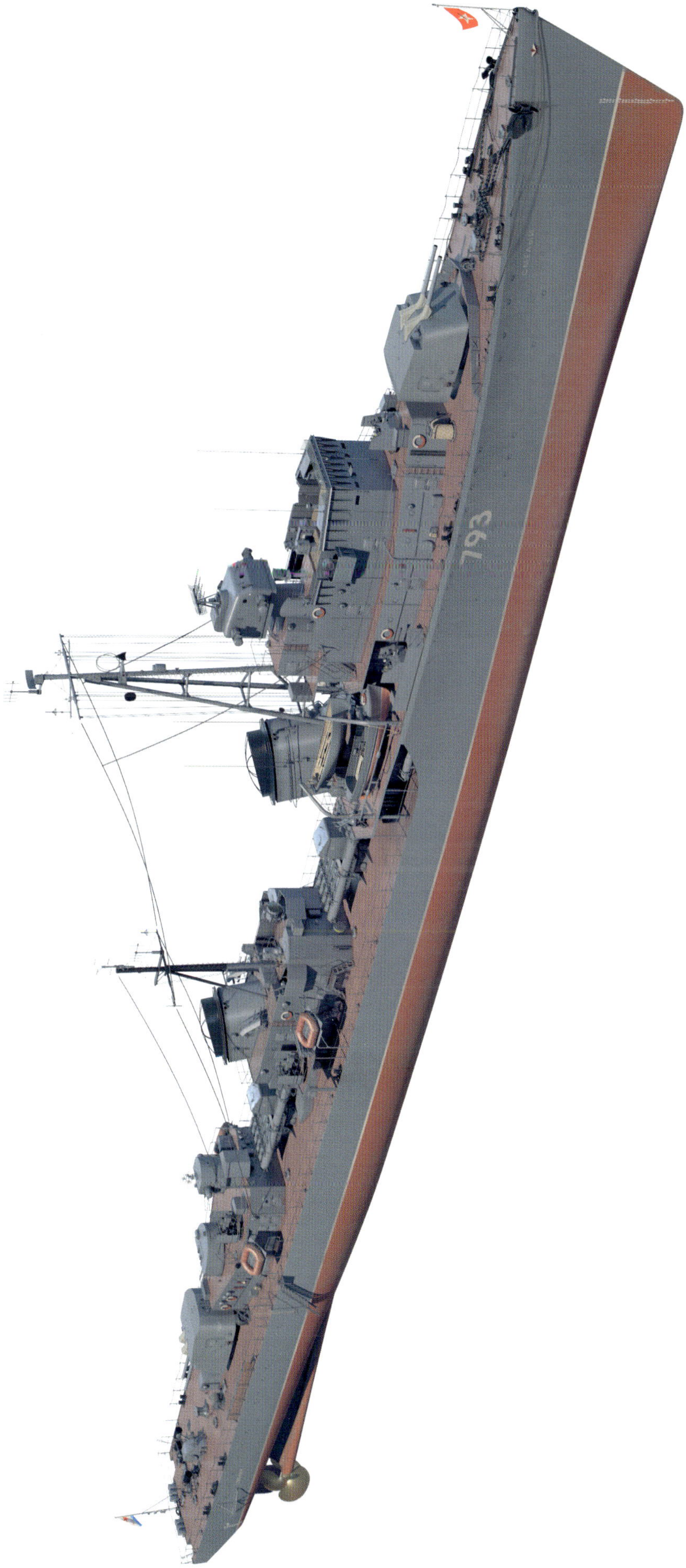

Overall view of the ship.

NAVAL ARCHIVES

Inside you will find:

INTERESTING ARTICLES

ARCHIVAL PHOTOS

DRAWINGS

3D ILLUSTRATIONS AND DRAWINGS OF THE FAMOUS WARSHIPS

ANAGLYPH 3D

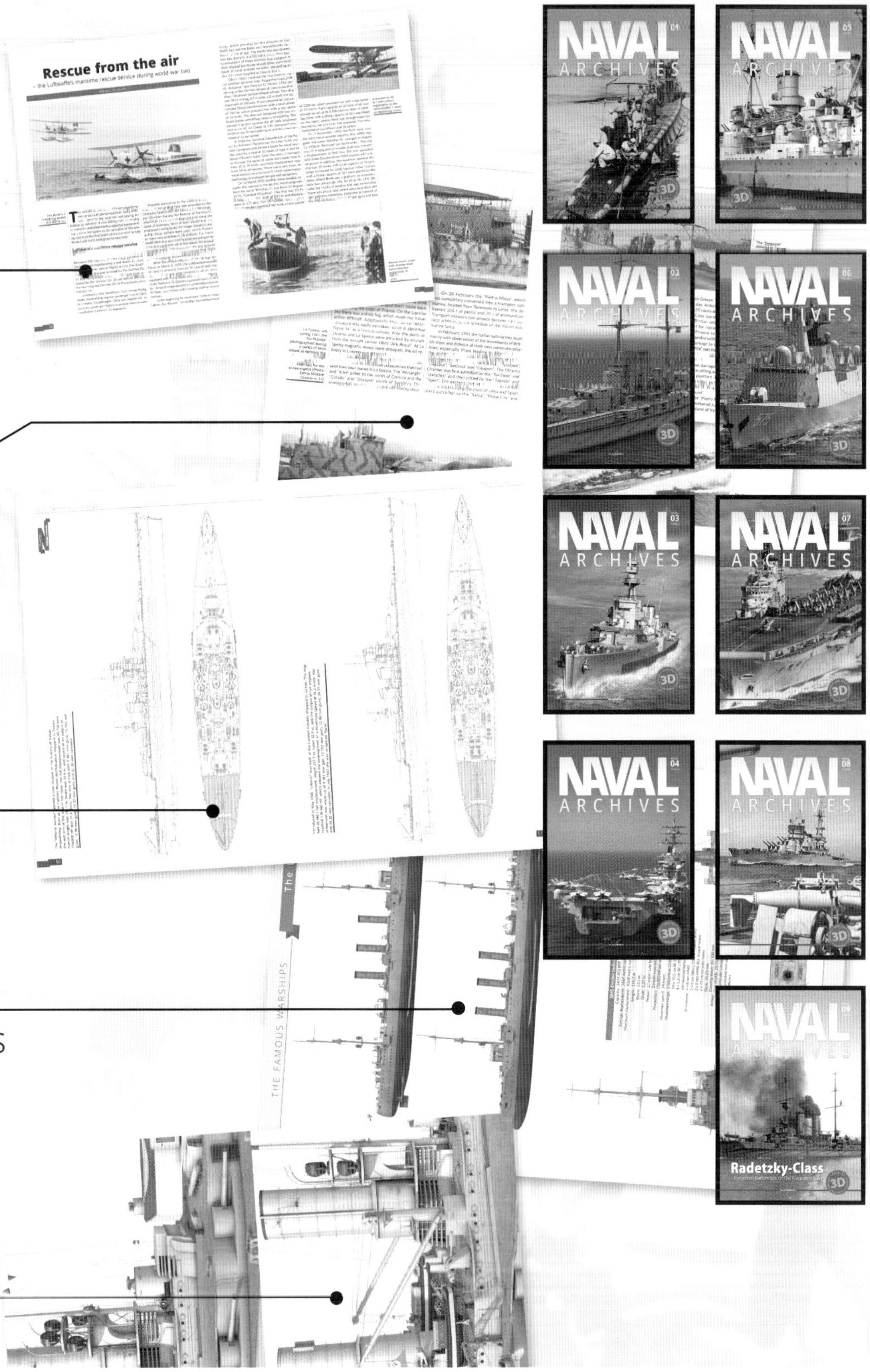

Visit our shop online **shop.kagero.pl**

The Soviet Skoryi Class Destroyer – Oleg Pomoshnikov

LUBLIN 2019 • ISBN 978-83-66148-30-7

© All rights reserved. With the exception of quoting brief passages for the purposes of review, no part of this publication may be reproduced without prior written permission from the Publisher. **Printed in Poland**

3D illustrations and captions, text: **Oleg Pomoshnikov** • Design: **KAGERO STUDIO** – Łukasz Maj

KAGERO Publishing • www.kagero.pl, e-mail: kagero@kagero.pl, marketing@kagero.pl

Editorial office, Marketing, Distribution: KAGERO Publishing, Akacjowa 100, os. Borek, Turka, 20-258 Lublin 62, Poland, phone/fax (+48) 81 501 21 05

www.kagero.eu

3D visualisations are based on the available photographs, drawings and other archive data, and should be treated only as author's attempt to recreate the original look of the particular machine as faithfully as possible. If you are in possession of materials to which author did not reach, and you would like to help us to develop a better publication, please contact the Publisher on: redakcja@kagero.pl